KiDS' TREATS

KiDS' TREATS

50 Easy, Extra-Special Snacks to Make with Your Little Ones

Katie Wyllie
madetobeamomma.com

A **adams**media

Avon, Massachusetts

Published by
Adams Media, a division of F+W Media, Inc.
57 Littlefield Street, Avon, MA 02322. U.S.A.
www.adamsmedia.com

ISBN 10: 1-4405-8964-X
ISBN 13: 978-1-4405-8964-5
eISBN 10: 1-4405-8965-8
eISBN 13: 978-1-4405-8965-2

Printed in the United States of America.

10   9   8   7   6   5   4   3   2   1

Library of Congress Cataloging-in-Publication Data

Wyllie, Katie.
  Kids' treats / Katie Wyllie.
     pages cm
  Includes index.
  ISBN 978-1-4405-8964-5 (pb) -- ISBN 1-4405-8964-X (pb) -- ISBN 978-1-4405-8965-2
(ebook) -- ISBN 1-4405-8965-8 (ebook)
  1. Desserts. 2. Cookies. 3. Cupcakes. 4. Candy. 5. Children--Nutrition. I. Title.
  TX773.W95 2015
  641.86--dc23

                                 2015012543

Always follow safety and commonsense cooking protocol while using kitchen utensils, operating ovens and stoves, and handling uncooked food. If children are assisting in the preparation of any recipe, they should always be supervised by an adult.

Many of the designations used by manufacturers and sellers to distinguish their products are claimed as trademarks. Where those designations appear in this book and F+W Media, Inc. was aware of a trademark claim, the designations have been printed with initial capital letters.

Cover design by Sylvia McArdle.
Cover images by Katie Wyllie.
Photography by Katie Wyllie.

This book is available at quantity discounts for bulk purchases.
For information, please call 1-800-289-0963.

DEDICATION

To my two little boys, Jacob and Carter, and any future children we may have. I am so blessed to be your momma and I am so thankful I have the privilege of making these treats with you. You are my absolute biggest blessings in life. You are my joy and my laughter. Love you always, Mommy.

ACKNOWLEDGMENTS

I would like to thank my friends, family, and readers that were so supportive of this book. Thank you to my wonderful husband, Bryan. Bryan, I appreciate all the encouragement through my blogging and book adventures. You are always my biggest fan. Thank you to my parents, particularly my mom, who taught me the value of homemaking. Mom, thank you for the hours you spent brainstorming with me and creating treats with me. Thank you to my grandparents, who always support everything I do. Thanks for the helping hands and for babysitting my two little boys when deadlines and projects were due. Thank you to my brother and three sisters. Aaron, thank you for your love and support. Faith, thank you for your excitement, encouragement, and last-minute Dunkin' Donuts runs when I just needed a break. Ashlea, thank you for the hours you spent with me helping me create recipes and ideas. Courtney, thank you for your online photography tips, support, and for always encouraging me in everything I do, no matter how far away you are. Lastly, thank you to all my *Made to Be a Momma* readers. I feel so honored to have "met" you through blogging and your constant support is always overwhelming. Thanks for all of the love.

CONTENTS

Preface 11

Introduction 13

Chapter 1

TIPS, TRICKS, AND TECHNIQUES   14

Buttercream Frosting 19

Cookie Glaze Icing 21

Perfect Chocolate Cupcakes 22

Sugar Cookies 25

Basic Oreo Bonbons 26

Chapter 2

UNDER THE SEA TREATS   28

Oreo Crabs 29

Underwater Gelatin Mason Jars 32

Oreo Frogs 35

Oreo Turtles 37

Pirate Oreos 40

Boat Cupcakes 43

Beachy Creamsicle Cupcakes 47

Cinnamon Sugar Tortilla Fish 49

Chapter 3

UNDER THE BIG TOP CIRCUS SNACKS   52

Balloon Sugar Cookies 53

Lion Crackers and Cheese 56

Circus Party Popcorn 59

Cotton Candy Cone Sugar Cookies 61

Monkey Oreo Bonbons 63

Rainbow Coated Pretzels 66

Colorful Yogurt Dots 69

Chapter 4

STORY TIME SNACKS   71

Cat in the Hat Cookies 73

Sheep Cupcakes 75

Princess Wand Sugar Cookie Sticks 77

Pilgrim Hats 80

Turkey Veggie Cup 83

Nutter Butter Ice Cream Cones 84

Fruit Rainbow Cup 87

Graham Cracker Airplane 89

Oreo Puppies 91

Oreo Hedgehogs 93

Valentine's Day Lollipops 97

Chapter 5

SPOOKY BITES — 98

Candy Corn Marshmallows 99
Monster Marshmallows 102
Ghost Sugar Cookies 105
Monster Rice Cereal Treats 106
Frankenstein Graham Crackers 109
Witch Cupcakes 110

Chapter 6

PICNIC MUNCHIES — 112

Oreo Bumblebees 113
Peanut Butter Cup Butterflies 117
Baby Chicks 118
Ice Cream Sandwiches 121
Watermelon Cupcakes 124
Flowerpot Cupcakes 127
Sports Balls Oreo Truffles 128
Easter Egg Nests 131
Peanut Butter Ritz Bunnies 133

Chapter 7

SNOWBALL FIGHT TREATS — 136

Santa Hats 137
Christmas Tree Brownies 141
Rice Cereal Ornaments 143
Snowflake Cupcakes 145
Gingerbread Cookies 147
Snowman Cupcakes 151
Oreo Penguins 153
Polar Bear Oreos 155
Love Bug Oreos 159

Appendix

U.S./Metric Conversion Charts 160
Index 165

PREFACE

Welcome! First of all, can I just say a "thank you" and an "I am so happy you are here!" When I first pursued writing this book, I had doubts that anyone would even want to read it. I felt the same way when I started my blog, *Made to Be a Momma*, but what I have learned over time is that we as women crave fellowship with other wives and moms who are just like us! I couldn't believe the response on *Made to Be a Momma* when I started sharing family recipes and stories of my crazy life. There is a constant need and desire to create with our children to help their imaginations flourish and form lasting memories for the few years we have them in our arms. *Kids' Treats* is filled with nostalgic thoughts of my childhood and the special memories I have made by creating with my children so far.

Growing up, I always loved all things crafts and recipes. I remember many afternoons spent with my grandmother that were filled with heading to the store to purchase fabric, carefully cutting out the fabric, and then sewing skirts, pillowcases, purses, and more! She has spent countless hours sharing her talents with me and this is something that I truly cherish. Many afternoons and evenings were also spent cleaning up the kitchen and making meals and desserts with my mother for our family of seven. My mom is a superhero of sorts and has always taught her children the value of homemaking. She is extremely talented in the kitchen and I am thankful she passed a few of those genes on to me. Readers of *Made to Be a Momma* know that I like to keep things simple in life. I may not always be making things from scratch, but I do love to add my own twist to recipes and make something my whole family will enjoy. Now that I am a mother of two crazy and rambunctious little boys, I have made it my goal to pass on some of the tips and tricks my grandmother and mother taught me, and nothing brings me greater joy than seeing my boys wearing their little aprons with a whisk or spatula in hand. My hope is that this cookbook will inspire you to cook, bake, and create with the little ones whom you love most. Creating with your children may be a little messy, but I promise the smiles and memories you will capture will be worth it. One day I hope my sons and any future children I have will share their memories with their families and that this tradition will continue on from generation to generation.

With my love,
Katie

INTRODUCTION

Do you love to watch your kids play and create in the kitchen? Do they get excited when you pull out baking ingredients and the stand mixer? Do you love seeing their faces when you help them make something that your whole family is excited to enjoy? Now, with *Kids' Treats* you can make the food that comes out of your kitchen as fun as the time you spend making it!

Filled with fifty sweet and savory treats, this book will keep you *and* your kids smiling for hours. Watch your little ones' creativity soar as they go sailing with the Pirate Oreos in Chapter 2, celebrate summer with the Peanut Butter Cup Butterflies in Chapter 6, or settle in for sleep with the adorable Sheep Cupcakes in Chapter 4. You'll even find recipes that will help you celebrate your favorite holidays, like the Frankenstein Graham Crackers in Chapter 5, the Turkey Veggie Cup in Chapter 4, and the Christmas Tree Brownies in Chapter 7.

Most of these treats are made in small batches—which makes them perfect when your kids are looking to do something fun at home—but you should feel free to double, triple, or even halve these recipes depending on where you'll be serving them. These treats are perfect for birthday parties, family gatherings, school functions, or even for adult get-togethers like baby showers or anniversary or holiday parties, so do what you have to do to make the recipes work for you and your family.

In addition to the kids' treats found throughout the book, you'll also find a chapter that educates you on the tools you need to successfully make these snacks. Here, you'll find info on common kitchen equipment and techniques that will make cooking easier—and stress free!—as well as some basic recipes for items like Buttercream Frosting, Cookie Glaze Icing, Sugar Cookies, and more that you'll find used again and again throughout the book. Fortunately, all the materials and ingredients used to make these amazing kids' treats are easy to find at your local supermarket or craft store or online, which means you can make whichever treat you or your kids crave, whenever you want. So grab your kids and get ready to have fun with your food! Enjoy!

Chapter 1

TIPS, TRICKS, AND TECHNIQUES

Before you start creating the food that's fun for you and your kids, you need to know what you should have on hand. In this chapter you'll find information on the kitchen tools—like a candy melting electric pot, disposable cake-decorating bags, and a cake-decorating paint set—that will help make creating these kids' treats fun and easy. You'll also find a variety of basic recipes that you'll see used over and over again throughout the following chapters. These recipes will give you the knowledge you need to whip through the serious cooking part of the process and get right to the fun! Also, while these tools and recipes are recommended, if you want to mix it up and do your own thing, go for it! If you want to use a fork to dip your cookies in melted chocolate instead of buying a dipping scoop, that's fine! If you want to use your grandma's sugar cookie recipe instead of the one that you'll find here, that's great! Do whatever works for you and your family, but don't forget to have fun, no matter what!

{ Favorite Kitchen Tools }

Creating and baking in the kitchen with your kids may be
a bit messy at times but it doesn't need to be stressful! In
this section you will find some of my favorite go-to kitchen
tools to have on hand while creating amazing snacks and
desserts with my kids. These simple tools not only make
creating treats easier and minimize messes, but many of
them, such as the Silpat and cookie scoop, can also be used
in everyday baking and cooking, which means that your

money will be well spent. That said, you do not *have* to
have these kitchen tools available, but they really do make
the time in the kitchen a bit easier. And since easy is so
important when you're a parent, you can find all of these
kitchen tools in your local craft store, online, and even in
your local grocery store.

So what should you have close by whenever you sit down
to make delicious treats with your family? Read on!

CANDY MELTS

Candy melts—small, medallion-shaped chocolate pieces that you can melt to cover cookies, cupcakes, and more in fun, delicious colors—are such a fun way to add something extra sweet and special to your treats. They come in many different colors and flavors and are simple to find online, in your local craft store, or even in some grocery stores. They easily melt in a candy melting electric pot or in the microwave, which makes treat making a breeze! I love to use the Wilton brand medallions because I think they melt the best. If you are having a bit of trouble with the chocolate melting, however, just add a tablespoon of canola or vegetable oil and stir. It should help smooth out the consistency of your chocolate medallions.

CANDY MELTING ELECTRIC POT

A candy melting electric pot is my favorite kids' treat decorating tool! It's basically a small, insulated pot that you plug into the wall (which means fewer dishes and easy cleanup!) and use to melt your candy melts. These pots have two temperatures, one that melts the chocolate and one that keeps it warm while you are making your dipped or decorated treats. You can find candy melting pots in any craft store (some even sell disposable versions) or online. I have even seen them in my local grocery stores. I prefer to use this method over microwaving my candy melts because the chocolate stays melted and I don't have to constantly reheat it when it starts to harden, but you can certainly use the microwave to melt your chocolates if you'd prefer.

CANDY MELT DIPPING SCOOP

A candy melt dipping scoop is a great tool for scooping and dipping the various treats you will be making easily into melted chocolate. It is a fancy wired slotted spoon that helps excess chocolate drip back into the bowl or melting pot, which makes treat making easier and less messy. I find that having a couple dipping scoops on hand is helpful if you're making different-colored treats, but one will do just fine. You can find these scoops online or in your local craft stores.

COOKIE SCOOP

A cookie scoop is another one of my favorite kitchen tools to have on hand. Similar to an ice cream scoop, a cookie scoop has a handle that you squeeze to push all of the cookie dough out of the scoop and onto your plate, baking sheet, or Silpat. It's great for shaping bonbons, scooping cookie batter, and even shaping some savory foods. For the treats you will find throughout this book, I recommend using a 1-inch cookie scoop, since it makes the perfect-sized treats.

DISPOSABLE CAKE-DECORATING BAGS

These cake-decorating bags—cone-shaped plastic bags that hold icing, frosting, or dough and a decorating tip—are great assistants to use when you're decorating your kids' treats. Using decorating bags results in less mess and cleaner lines then trying to do intricate decorating with spoons or toothpicks. I like to use disposable bags for easy cleanup but you can also use the reusable, polyester bags if you'd prefer. To place the frosting in the bag, fold the top edge over about 2–3 inches, then scoop your icing into the bag with a spoon. Once the icing is in the bag, just fold the top edges back up and twist the top of the decorating bag to remove air. Cut off the tip of the bag. This process helps keep the edges of the bag clean.

CAKE-DECORATING TIPS

Cake-decorating tips—metal or plastic tips that you place inside the decorating bag to change the way the frosting or icing looks on your treat—are a fun way to add designs to your Oreo treats, cupcakes, and more! My favorite decorating tip sizes are 1M, 1, 2, and 4 and you'll see these sizes used frequently throughout the recipes in the book when it's time to add the finishing touches to the treats you will be making.

COUPLERS

Couplers are small, two-piece, cake-decorating devices that allow you to change your cake-decorating tips without having to change the bag. I use these when I want to use the same icing color but want multiple designs. These can be helpful when decorating kids' treats but are not necessary. If you do decide to use a coupler, insert the larger of the two pieces inside the cake-decorating bag and push it down into the bag's tip. Use a pen to mark a spot in the middle of the coupler's threads, then use scissors to cut off the top of the bag at that mark, and return the coupler to the bottom of the bag. Next, flip the bag over and add your chosen decorating tip to the top of the coupler, making sure to keep the tip outside of the bag so it's easy to change out as needed. Then, take the unused, circular piece of the coupler and screw it over the decorating tip to secure it to the bag.

SPRINKLES

Sprinkles are my go-to embellishing tools when creating fun treats for kids. I love to use the round rainbow sprinkles, but I also like to have colors such as brown, pink, blue, green, and more in stock. Use sprinkles to add color and texture to your treats and you're guaranteed to have happy kids—every time!

SILICONE BAKING SHEETS OR PARCHMENT PAPER

Silicone baking sheets or parchment paper are great to use when baking or transferring treats. I prefer to use a Silpat, a nonstick, silicone surface that lies over a cookie sheet and can be used for both baking and cooking. A Silpat is a great tool when decorating treats, makes for easy transfer from refrigerator to counter, and ensures that cleanup is a breeze. If you decide to use a Silpat or other silicon baking sheet, be sure to avoid cutting anything on the mat as the blade of a knife or pizza cutter can cut right through, destroying the mat. Also, if you don't have or want to use a silicone baking sheet, you can use parchment paper in the same way.

CAKE-DECORATING PAINT SET

The brushes in a cake-decorating paint set are used to paint details, facial features, and designs on your kids' treats. For example, you can use the bottom of the paintbrushes to create eyes and polka dots. You can also use a toothpick for your designing, but paintbrushes create a much smoother and cleaner look. You can find these paintbrushes online and in the cake-decorating sections of your local crafts stores.

GEL ICING COLORS

Gel icing colors are a fun way to add some color to your kids' favorite treats! A thicker version of the liquid food coloring that you may have grown up with, these give you an array of colors that will match any party or occasion. I use gel colors because the colors are brighter than liquid colors and the consistency is the same as icing. I personally like to use the AmeriColor and Wilton brands that you can find in your local craft stores and online. I like all the color options these two brands offer as well as the brightness of the colors.

{ Basic Recipes }

Many of the kids' treats you will create with your little ones start with a basic recipe base. In this section, you'll find a collection of some delicious recipes that you will use to make the treats found throughout the book. But while these basic recipes are used over and over again in the following chapters, they're meant to be starting points for you and the little ones' creativity. If you prefer vanilla over chocolate, feel free to make the switch! Also, all of these recipes can be made in halves, quarters, or can even be doubled depending on how many treats you want to make. I tend to halve most of these basic recipes when making treats for my two little ones, but do what works best for you and your family.

{ Buttercream Frosting }

This classic buttercream frosting is sweet and delicious and it's the perfect icing for cupcakes, cakes, and cookies!
I love using the #1M cake-decorating tip when piping this frosting. It gives the cupcakes such a pretty peak.
You can also use a small spatula and spread this icing over a cake. But however you're using this
Buttercream Frosting, just add a few drops of your favorite gel icing colors and you can
match the color scheme for any party or special occasion!

YIELDS 3 CUPS FROSTING

2 sticks butter, softened

4 cups powdered sugar, divided, plus
  2–3 tablespoons as needed

2 teaspoons vanilla extract

1 tablespoon milk, plus 2–3 tablespoons if needed

1. In a large mixing bowl, whisk together butter and 1 cup powdered sugar.

2. Add vanilla extract and milk and slowly add remaining powdered sugar.
Mix until combined.

3. Take a spatula and run it through your frosting to form small peaks. If the peaks keep their shape and don't fall over it's stiff enough to pipe. If the peaks fall over, add more powdered sugar, about 1 tablespoon at a time. Continue to add either milk or powdered sugar until desired consistency is met.

4. If storing, place in an airtight container and place on counter for up to 2 weeks. If using right away, place frosting in a cake-decorating bag with a #1M cake-decorating tip or tip of your choice.

5. Working from the outside in, pipe your frosting in a circular motion until you have a small peak of icing.

{ Cookie Glaze Icing }

This sugary confection is great for embellishing cookies and treats! It has a delicious sweet flavor, which makes it the perfect pairing for my favorite Sugar Cookie recipe (see recipe in this chapter). You can swap out the water in this recipe for milk for a shinier glaze or use water for a more matte glaze.

YIELDS ENOUGH TO ICE ABOUT 2 DOZEN
MEDIUM-SIZED COOKIES

1 pound powdered sugar (3¾ cups), plus 2–3 tablespoons as needed

¼ cup corn syrup, plus 2–3 tablespoons as needed

½ teaspoon vanilla extract

¼ teaspoon almond extract

¼ cup water

2–3 drops AmeriColor icing gel or Wilton icing gel, your desired colors

1. Mix together all ingredients with an electric mixer on low speed until fully incorporated. Add more powdered sugar or corn syrup 1 teaspoon at a time until proper consistency is met. Icing shouldn't run once piped onto cookie.

2. Once your icing is the correct consistency, lay a piece of cling wrap on the counter. Pour icing in the middle of the cling wrap.

3. Wrap the icing in the cling wrap by folding the cling wrap on top of itself. Grab both ends of the cling wrap and swing it like a jump rope. This ensures that the ends of the cling wrap roll up nice and tight.

4. Take one end of the tightly twisted ends and string it through the cake-decorating bag. I add a coupler first so I can change out the tips as needed but a coupler is not necessary if you are only using one tip. Using a pair of scissors, snip the twisted end and add your cake-decorating tip. You are now ready to decorate. If you will not be decorating right away, store your filled cake-decorating bags with the tips upright and covered in plastic wrap in the refrigerator. I put my bags in a mug or cup so they don't tip over. Use refrigerated icing within 1 week.

{ Perfect Chocolate Cupcakes }

My husband loves chocolate cupcakes and cakes. It's his number one choice and his chocolate-loving taste buds have been passed down to our two little boys. These Perfect Chocolate Cupcakes are soft, rich, moist, and chocolaty—everything you or your kids could possibly want in a chocolate cupcake! If you don't want cupcakes, you can also make this recipe into two 9-inch cakes that are perfect for birthday parties!

YIELDS 24 CUPCAKES OR TWO 9-INCH CAKES

2 cups flour	2 teaspoons baking powder	1 cup vegetable oil	1 cup cold water
2 cups sugar	¾ cup cocoa powder	2 eggs	
2 teaspoons baking soda	½ teaspoon salt	1 cup boiling water	

1. Preheat oven to 350°F.

2. Mix together all ingredients in a large bowl until combined.

3. Place cake into a greased 9" × 13" pan, two 9-inch cake pans, or two cupcake pans.

4. Bake for 25 minutes or until a fork inserted into the middle of the cake or cupcakes comes out clean. Allow cake or cupcakes to cool completely before icing. Cover iced cupcakes or cake with plastic wrap or store in an airtight container for 2–3 days.

{ Sugar Cookies }

What do you want in a sugar cookie? No chilling required. Perfect edges every time. Crunchy on the outside and soft on the inside. These moist and delicious Sugar Cookies fit the bill! The nutmeg in this recipe adds a fun pop of flavor and the cornstarch helps keep the cookies' shape. Delicious!

YIELDS APPROXIMATELY 3 DOZEN COOKIES

2 cups cold butter, cubed

1½ cups sugar

½ teaspoon sea salt

2 eggs

1½ teaspoons vanilla extract

4¼ cups flour, plus ¼ cup as needed

½ cup cornstarch

¼ teaspoon nutmeg

½ cup sour cream

1. Preheat oven to 375°F.

2. Cream together butter, sugar, and salt in a stand mixer with paddle attachment.

3. Mix in the eggs and vanilla extract.

4. Add flour, cornstarch, and nutmeg. Mix on low until fully incorporated.

5. Stir in the sour cream.

6. Use a rolling pin to roll all of the cookie dough out to a thickness of ¼ inch. You may also work with half of the dough at a time if needed. If your cookie dough is sticky you may lightly flour your surface. Cut cookie dough into desired shapes using your favorite cookie cutters.

7. Bake for 10 minutes or until edges are lightly browned. Do not overbake. Remove from oven. If decorating right away, allow cookies to cool completely before icing. If storing, place them in an airtight container for up to 2 weeks or in the freezer for a few months.

{ Basic Oreo Bonbons }

This classic Oreo Bonbon recipe makes for the perfect "pop-in-your-mouth" treat for kids and adults! My favorite Oreo cookie to use is the Double Stuf Oreo cookie but any of your favorites would work great! You can top your bonbons with crushed peanuts, sprinkles, or even drizzle some melted chocolate on top.

YIELDS APPROXIMATELY 2-3 DOZEN BONBONS,
DEPENDING ON WHAT SIZE YOU MAKE

1 package Oreo cookies
8-ounce package full-fat cream cheese, softened
1-pound bag light cocoa candy melts

1. Finely crush Oreos in a food processor. Then, place Oreos in a medium-sized bowl and mix cookie mixture with cream cheese until combined.

2. Scoop cookie mixture with a 1-inch cookie scoop.

3. Place cookie bonbons on a cookie sheet lined with parchment paper or a Silpat. Chill in the refrigerator for 30 minutes.

4. While chilling, melt cocoa candy melts in a candy melting electric pot according to package instructions, or in the microwave for 30-second increments.

5. Dip chilled Oreo balls, using a candy melt dipping scoop or fork, into the melted chocolate, making sure to cover the whole bonbon. If sprinkles or toppings are desired, add them now while the chocolate is still warm.

6. Put chocolate-covered bonbons back into the refrigerator until chocolate hardens, approximately 20 minutes.

Chapter 2

UNDER THE SEA TREATS

Oreo Crabs

Underwater Gelatin Mason Jars

Oreo Frogs

Oreo Turtles

Pirate Oreos

Boat Cupcakes

Beachy Creamsicle Cupcakes

Cinnamon Sugar Tortilla Fish

{ Oreo Crabs }

Make those crabby sea creatures come to life by whipping up these fun and bright Oreo Crabs. Your kids will be ready for a day at the beach and, since these sweet treats are so easy to make, you'll be heading out the door in no time! These Oreo Crabs are also perfect for birthday parties, baby showers, or any day when your family is ready to relax and catch a few rays!

YIELDS 6 OREO CRABS

½ cup red chocolate candy melts
2 red Pull 'n' Peel Twizzlers
6 Oreo cookies

12 candy eyes
Red sprinkles, optional
¼ cup yellow candy melts, optional

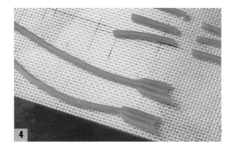

1. Melt your red candy melts in a candy melting electric pot according to the package instructions, or in the microwave at 30-second increments.

2. Pull one Pull 'n' Peel string from your Twizzler and cut it into six small pieces to use for legs.

3. Place three of the small leg pieces about ¼ inch away from each other in parallel lines on a Silpat or wax paper–lined cookie sheet. Repeat the same step with the remaining three leg pieces about 1 inch from the other set of legs.

4. Pull three Pull 'n' Peel strings from your Twizzlers. Cut two diagonal lines toward the middle of these three Twizzlers to create a claw shape. Remove the remaining two strings.

(Continued on next page) ▶

5. Dip Oreo in melted chocolate and fully cover with chocolate. Using a fork or candy melt dipping scoop, tap lightly to remove any excess chocolate from the Oreo.

6. Place chocolate-covered Oreo on top of the three legs. Add claw pieces to either side of your Oreo, lightly pressing the Twizzler into the melted chocolate. Place eyeballs on top toward the front of your Oreo. Add sprinkles to the Oreo behind the eyes. If desired, melt yellow candy melts and use a cake-decorating paintbrush or toothpick to paint a small mouth on the front of your Oreo.

7. Repeat with additional Oreos, then place crabs in refrigerator until hardened, approximately 20 minutes.

TREAT TIPS!

You can find candy eyes online or in your local craft store in the baking department.

Underwater Gelatin Mason Jars

Sure to impress any under-the-sea lovers, the addition of Swedish Fish to these Underwater Gelatin Mason Jars adds a fun twist to a classic gelatin treat. Pour your gelatin into pint-sized mason jars and screw on the top for a fun and delicious on-the-go picnic snack during the summer.
And be sure to remember the whipped topping. It's the best part!

YIELDS 4 PINT-SIZED MASON JARS

1 (3-ounce) box blue raspberry or lime green gelatin
4 pint-sized mason jars

1 (12-ounce) container whipped topping such as Cool Whip
1 (2-ounce) bag Swedish Fish

1. Prepare gelatin according to package instructions.

2. Pour gelatin into mason jars.

3. Place gelatin-filled mason jars into refrigerator until gelatin has completely set, about 4 hours.

4. Add a dollop of whipped topping and place a Swedish Fish on top.

{ Oreo Frogs }

These Oreo Frogs are the very first kids' treat I ever created with my oldest son Jacob.
He was so proud when we were done and your child is sure to feel the same! Kids just love the frog's
silly tongue and this Oreo Frog recipe is a personal—and a reader—favorite!

YIELDS 6 OREO FROGS

1 cup green chocolate candy melts
1 red Starburst candy
6 Oreo cookies
12 tiny twist pretzels
Green sprinkles, optional

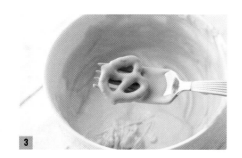

1. Melt your chocolate candy melts in a candy melting electric pot according to the package instructions, or in the microwave at 30-second increments.

2. Cut a ½-inch, tongue-shaped piece out of the Starburst with a butter knife or kitchen scissors.

3. Dip Oreos and pretzels in melted chocolate with candy melt dipping scoop or fork and cover completely with chocolate.

(Continued on next page) ▶

4. Remove from bowl and place pretzels side by side, bottoms touching, on top of a piece of parchment paper or Silpat.

5. Place chocolate-covered Oreo on top of pretzels.

6. While the chocolate is still warm add the red tongue piece to the center front of the Oreo. Then, place the eyes on top of Oreo and add sprinkles to the cookie.

7. Place frogs in the refrigerator until chocolate hardens, approximately 20 minutes.

{ Oreo Turtles }

T is for Turtle. A fun way to teach children their letters is by designating a different letter for each day. These little guys are perfect for "T" day! Turtles aren't known for being very fast but you will be able to put together these fun kids' treats in no time!

YIELDS 6 OREO TURTLES

1 cup green candy melts
6 Oreo cookies
1 tube of green gel icing
Green sprinkles, optional
¼–½ cup graham cracker crumbs, optional

1. Melt green candy melts in a candy melting electric pot according to package instructions, or in the microwave at 30-second increments.

2. Dip your Oreo cookies into the melted chocolate using a candy melt dipping scoop or fork and cover completely. Place in refrigerator until chocolate hardens, approximately 5 minutes.

3. Using the melted chocolate and small cake-decorating paintbrushes, paint six turtle heads about 1 inch long and ½ inch wide and twelve fins that are ½ inch long on a piece of parchment paper. Place in refrigerator until chocolate hardens, approximately 2–3 minutes.

(Continued on next page) ▶

4. Attach the fins and head of the turtle to the bottom of the dipped Oreo cookies, using your cake-decorating paintbrushes and melted chocolate as a glue.

5. Place turtles on Silpat or parchment paper and place in refrigerator until chocolate has hardened, approximately 5 minutes.

6. Using the green gel icing, pipe a turtle shell design on the top of each turtle's back. Top with sprinkles if you desire.

7. If desired, lay your graham cracker crumbs on a plate or platter and use the crumbs as a fun way to display the Oreo Turtles in the sand.

{ Pirate Oreos }

"Arrggh, Matey!" Let your kids put on their best swashbuckling act with these adorable Pirate Oreo friends. You can easily change the colors of the bandannas to make pirates that are perfect for a party of any color scheme. To really set the mood, place some Rolos in a bowl nearby for some fun gold treasure.

YIELDS 6 PIRATE OREOS

1 cup white chocolate candy melts
6 Oreos
¼ cup red chocolate candy melts
¼ cup green chocolate candy melts
¼ cup brown chocolate candy melts

1. Melt your white chocolate candy melts in a candy melting electric pot according to the package instructions, or in the microwave at 30-seconds increments.

2. Dip Oreos in white chocolate with candy melt dipping scoop or fork and cover completely. Place Oreos on parchment paper or Silpat and refrigerate until chocolate is hardened, approximately 10 minutes.

3. In three separate bowls, melt your red, green, and brown chocolate melts in the microwave at 30-second increments. Remove chocolate-covered Oreos from refrigerator and keep them on the Silpat.

4. Using a small cake-decorating paintbrush and either the red or green melted candy melts, "paint" on a pirate hat by painting a straight line about ¼ of the way down from the top of the Oreo. Then use the same color to fill in the empty space above the line until the Oreo is colored up to the rounded top edge.

(Continued on next page) ▶

5. Place Oreos back in refrigerator until hat hardens, approximately 5 minutes.

6. Using your melted chocolate and small cake-decorating paintbrushes, paint small ties, the same colors as your pirate hats, on top of your parchment paper or Silpat. Place in refrigerator until small-tie chocolate hardens, approximately 2–3 minutes.

7. Remove ties from refrigerator and using a small amount of melted candy melts attach a tie to the right or left side of each pirate's hat.

8. Using your remaining melted chocolate and the bottom edge of a small cake-decorating paintbrush, add polka dots to the pirate hat. Continuing to use the bottom end of your paintbrushes, add eyes, a nose, a smile, and two small lines to create your pirate's hair.

9. Place Oreos in refrigerator until all chocolate is hardened, approximately 5 minutes. Remove from refrigerator and enjoy!

{ Boat Cupcakes }

Let your kids sail away on a magical sea adventure with these fun and colorful Boat Cupcakes. You can create these boats with just a few simple craft supplies. The jute helps tie everything together and adds a fun nautical feel. Your kids will especially love the little fish popping out of the water!

YIELDS 2 DOZEN CUPCAKES

24 Perfect Chocolate Cupcakes (see recipe in Chapter 1) or cupcakes of your choice

1 batch Buttercream Frosting (see recipe in Chapter 1) colored with Wilton Sky Blue coloring gel

1 roll washi tape (any width), found in your local craft store

24 (6-inch) lollipop sticks (you can find these at your local craft store or online)

2 pieces of 12" × 12" brown scrapbooking paper

24 assorted colored Swedish Fish

24 (15-inch) cut pieces of jute or yarn, optional

1. Using a small spatula, frost cupcakes with the icing side to side to give it a wave effect.

2. Cut a 4-inch-long piece of washi tape. Place it at the top of the lollipop stick, then fold it over so the sticky ends meet. Cut a small triangle shape out of the end of your folded washi tape to create a flag.

3. Cut 24 boat shapes out of the brown scrapbooking paper. My boats were about 3 inches long and 2 inches high in the center.

(Continued on next page) ▶

4. Cut your Swedish Fish in half crosswise and add the front half of the Swedish Fish to the center of your cupcake.

5. Add your boat directly behind your Swedish Fish and the lollipop stick directly behind the boat and enjoy! Tie your jute or yarn around the cupcake wrapper to add a nautical feel.

TREAT TIPS!

Make sure the scrapbooking paper is a little bit heavier than construction paper so it will stand in the icing properly.

{ Beachy Creamsicle Cupcakes }

The flavors of these orange cupcakes topped with fun umbrellas will transport you and your kids' imaginations to an enjoyable summery oasis. The cream cheese frosting is just popping with flavor from the orange gelatin. If you don't like cream cheese frosting, feel free to swap it out with the classic Buttercream Frosting in Chapter 1.

YIELDS 16 CUPCAKES

CUPCAKES

2 cups flour

¼ teaspoon baking powder

¼ teaspoon baking soda

4 tablespoons orange gelatin powder

¼ teaspoon salt

½ cup butter, softened

1 cup sugar

2 large eggs

1 (8-ounce) can Crush orange soda

¼ cup milk

2 teaspoons orange extract

1 teaspoon vanilla extract

CREAMSICLE CREAM CHEESE FROSTING

4 ounces cream cheese, softened

¼ cup butter, softened

2½ cups powdered sugar

2 tablespoons orange gelatin powder

(Continued on next page) ▶

1. *For Cupcakes:* Preheat oven to 350°F. In a small bowl mix together flour, baking powder, baking soda, orange gelatin powder, and salt.

2. In a separate bowl, cream together butter, sugar, and eggs. Slowly add orange soda, milk, and orange and vanilla extracts. Mix until fully incorporated.

3. Pour mixture into paper-lined muffin tins ¾ full.

4. Bake for 20–22 minutes or until edges are lightly golden. Remove from oven and set aside to cool completely.

5. *For Creamsicle Cream Cheese Frosting:* Whisk together cream cheese, butter, powdered sugar, and orange gelatin powder.

6. Place icing in a cake-decorating bag with a #1M tip and pipe icing on cupcakes.

7. Top with little umbrellas that you can find at your local craft store if desired.

{ Cinnamon Sugar Tortilla Fish }

These fun, fish-shaped Cinnamon Sugar Tortillas are delicious! When my oldest son was turning three he rummaged through our bread drawer, brought out the tortillas, and asked to make his "sugary fish chips." They were a hit at our house and they'll be a hit at yours, too! These tortillas are delicious when served with fresh fruit but they also taste great with Nutella and peanut butter!

YIELDS 8–10 MEDIUM TO SMALL TORTILLA FISH

½ tablespoon cinnamon

2 tablespoons sugar

Fish cookie cutter or cookie cutter shape you desire

3 (8-inch or 10-inch) white flour tortillas

2 tablespoons melted butter

1 cup fresh diced fruit, optional

Nutella, optional

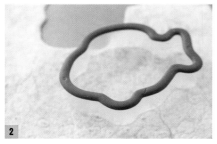

1. Preheat your oven to 350°F, then whisk together cinnamon and sugar in a small bowl.

2. Use your desired cookie cutters to cut shapes out of your white flour tortillas. Then place the tortillas on a silicone baking sheet or a piece of parchment paper.

3. Brush melted butter on top of your tortilla shapes, then sprinkle them with cinnamon and sugar mixture.

(Continued on next page) ▶

4. Place tortillas in the oven and bake for 7–10 minutes or until edges are lightly crisped. Remove from oven and allow to cool completely.

5. Once tortillas have cooled, dip your Cinnamon Sugar Tortillas in fruit, Nutella, or your desired topping.

TREAT TIPS!

If desired, you can put your tortillas in the microwave for 10–20 seconds to warm them up. It will help make it easier to cut them, especially for little hands.

Chapter 3

UNDER THE BIG TOP CIRCUS SNACKS

Balloon Sugar Cookies

Lion Crackers and Cheese

Circus Party Popcorn

Cotton Candy Cone Sugar Cookies

Monkey Oreo Bonbons

Rainbow Coated Pretzels

Colorful Yogurt Dots

{ Balloon Sugar Cookies }

Up, up, and away! Everyone remembers the excitement that went along with getting a balloon when they were a little kid! Those helium-filled favorites, in all the colors of the rainbow, are a circus mainstay and your kids probably look forward to getting them as much as you once did! Bring your kids back to the circus with these Balloon Sugar Cookies that are so much fun and super simple to make! All you need is my favorite Sugar Cookie recipe, a small balloon cookie cutter, and a batch of glaze icing. If you don't have a balloon cookie cutter a circle cutter will work just as great!

YIELDS 3 DOZEN COOKIES

1 batch Sugar Cookies (see recipe in Chapter 1) cut using a balloon or circle cookie cutter

1 batch Cookie Glaze Icing (see recipe in Chapter 1)

2–3 drops each of the following AmeriColor gels: Avocado (green balloons), Gold (yellow balloons), and a mixture of Sky Blue and Navy Blue (blue balloons)

1. Separate your icing into four bowls, adding only a small amount to one of the bowls. Color three of the bowls with your desired colors, making sure to leave the bowl with the least amount of icing white to create the highlight in your balloon.

2. Place each colored icing in a separate cake-decorating bag with a #2 tip.

3. To decorate your cookie, choose an icing color and use it to outline two cookies at a time with icing.

(Continued on next page) ▶

4. Go back and fill in the first cookie with the same color icing and then repeat with the second cookie. I like to only do two cookies at a time so the gel dries nicely and doesn't leave a ridge.

5. Repeat until all of your cookies have been iced with blue, green, or yellow icing.

6. Allow the icing to dry for about 4–5 hours and then add a small white highlight in the shape of a thick line on the top right-hand side of each balloon.

7. Let the Balloon Sugar Cookies air-dry on your counter until the icing has completely hardened, about 10 hours, then enjoy!

{ Lion Crackers and Cheese }

If you have a picky eater on your hands, you know that one way to get him to try new foods is by making it fun! We have a very picky eater in our family too and I am always trying to think of fun ways to plate my son's food. I think you'll find that this lion made with crackers and cheese is as big a hit in your home as it is in ours!

YIELDS ENOUGH CHEESE AND CRACKERS TO FEED 4-6 KIDS

8-ounce block Cheddar cheese

8-ounce block Colby-Jack cheese

1 slice of sandwich thins or a slice of bread cut into a circle shape

1 strawberry

1 tablespoon Nutella

1 sleeve Ritz crackers

1. Slice half a block of each kind of cheeses and set aside.

2. Place a slice of sandwich thin or bread on a plate.

3. Cut the bottom off a strawberry and place it on the piece of bread to create the lion's nose.

4. Using the Nutella and a small spoon, create two eyes, a mouth, and a few freckles on both sides of the nose.

5. Arrange crackers and cheese around the sandwich thin, alternating crackers and cheese.

{ Circus Party Popcorn }

Everybody loves the circus and, whether you're snuggling up on the couch to watch a circus-themed movie or are getting your kids excited to go to the real thing, this Circus Party Popcorn is the perfect snack! Anytime my kids hear the air pop popcorn machine they come running to the kitchen and giggle as they watch the popcorn pop into the bowl. Throw in some colorful Froot Loops and animal crackers and you're well on your way to serving up a fun, circus-friendly snack that your kids are sure to love!

YIELDS 5 CUPS CIRCUS PARTY POPCORN

3 cups popped popcorn, lightly salted and buttered
1 cup Froot Loops
1 cup animal crackers

Mix together the three ingredients and place in a small bowl. Serve immediately.

{ Cotton Candy Cone Sugar Cookies }

It's not a circus or day at the fair without a sweet cotton candy treat! Fortunately, these Cotton Candy Cone Sugar Cookies are perfect for any carnival-themed party! They're delicious and their classic blue and pink colors really set the stage for a fun day under the big top!

YIELDS 12 COTTON CANDY COOKIES

½ batch Buttercream Frosting (see recipe in Chapter 1)
2–3 drops Wilton Sky Blue coloring gel
2–3 drops Wilton Pink coloring gel

12 prepared sugar cookies, cut out using an ice cream cone cookie cutter
Rainbow sprinkles

1. Take your Buttercream Frosting and divide it evenly into three separate glass bowls. Use your food coloring to color two bowls of frosting until you have one bowl each of blue, pink, and white frosting. Note that the white frosting doesn't need any food coloring.

2. Using a small spatula, spread white icing on the bottom cone part of the ice cream cone cookie. Sprinkle rainbow sprinkles on top of the frosting.

(Continued on next page) ▶

3. Clean frosting off of spatula, then use it to spread pink icing and then blue icing on top of the ice cream cone cookie. Use your spatula to lightly pull up the icing to make it look fluffy like cotton candy really is!

TREAT TIPS!

If you'd like, feel free to add some cotton candy extract to the Buttercream Frosting. You can find it online at Amazon.com. But if you don't feel like taking this extra step, vanilla extract works just fine, too.

{ Monkey Oreo Bonbons }

When we found out our first baby was going to be a boy, I wanted a jungle-themed baby shower.

When we found out our second baby was another boy I wanted a little jungle-themed nursery.

And ever since my little boys were born their nicknames have been "my little monkeys." And just like my kids,

your little monkeys are guaranteed to love these Monkey Oreo Bonbons! Perfect for a circus party,

baby shower, or just a monkey birthday party, you're guaranteed to wish you had made more!

YIELDS 2 DOZEN MONKEY BONBONS

1 (1-pound) bag light cocoa candy melts

1 batch Basic Oreo Bonbons, completed through Step 3
(see recipe in Chapter 1)

1 cup butterscotch-flavored candy melts

48 butterscotch chips

1. Melt your cocoa candy melts in a candy melting electric pot according to the package instructions, or in the microwave at 30-second increments.

2. Dip the Basic Oreo Bonbons into the melted chocolate using a candy melt dipping scoop or fork and cover the bonbons completely.

3. Place chocolate-covered bonbons on a piece of parchment paper or Silpat. Place in refrigerator until chocolate hardens, about 10 minutes.

4. While the bonbons are chilling, melt butterscotch-flavored candy melts according to the package instructions, or in the microwave at 30-second increments.

5. Use the cake-decorating paintbrushes and butterscotch candy melts to paint the face and circular cheeks of the monkey onto the front center of the bonbon.

(Continued on next page) ▶

6. Use the cake-decorating paintbrushes to apply melted chocolate to the side of two butterscotch chips. Then attach the chips to both sides at the top of the bonbon for the monkey's ears. Place bonbons back in the refrigerator until chocolate hardens, about 5 minutes.

7. Once the chocolate is hard, use your cake-decorating paintbrushes to paint on the smile with the melted chocolate. Use the bottom end of your cake-decorating paintbrushes to create two dots for eyes and a short line for the nose. Place back in refrigerator until chocolate is completely hardened, approximately 2–3 minutes.

{ Rainbow Coated Pretzels }

Salty and sweet and oh-so-colorful, these Rainbow Coated Pretzels are just the thing to remind you of a fun, carefree day at the circus! You can package these pretzels in clear treat bags and tie them with a ribbon and they're perfect to pass out as favors at a circus-themed kids' party or even to bring to the circus itself! I love to use pretzel rods but if you prefer, you could use regular pretzels and completely dip them in your melted chocolate.

YIELDS 12 RAINBOW COATED PRETZELS

1 cup white chocolate candy melts
12 pretzel rods
¼ cup rainbow sprinkles

1. Melt chocolate candy melts in candy melting electric pot according to package instructions, or in a microwave at 30-second increments.

2. Dip pretzel rods halfway into the melted chocolate. Use a spoon to help cover pretzels if necessary.

3. Sprinkle the sprinkles onto the chocolate-coated pretzels while the chocolate is still hot.

4. Place your pretzels on a Silpat or parchment paper and place in refrigerator until chocolate hardens, approximately 10 minutes.

{ Colorful Yogurt Dots }

If your kids are anything like mine, they love yogurt and they also love fruit. So why not combine them and make an extra-special treat! These Colorful Yogurt Dots are the perfect bite of coolness during hot summer days when you and your kids are looking forward to a summer night spent under the big top at the circus or under the night sky at a local fair. And, what makes these treats even more amazing is that they're a healthy treat that's easy to grab while you're on the run! Easy for you *and* fun for your kids? What could be better?

YIELDS 1 CUP YOGURT ICE CREAM OR YOGURT BITES

1 (8-ounce) container vanilla yogurt
½ cup frozen blueberries
½ cup frozen raspberries

1. In an electric blender at high speed, blend together yogurt and frozen fruit until mixture is smooth and the consistency is of soft ice cream.

2. Scoop the yogurt/berry blend 1 teaspoon at a time into dots on parchment paper or Silpat and flatten lightly with a spoon or finger.

3. Flash-freeze yogurt dots in freezer until frozen, approximately 10 minutes.

4. Place in a container and keep in freezer for up to 2 weeks.

(Continued on next page) ▶

TREAT TIPS!

Even though I use blueberries and raspberries, feel free to use whatever kind of fruit you and your kids like. And, if you *do* use these berries, you can either blend them together to create one purple color or blend the colors separately to have purple dots and red dots. Rather than forming the yogurt mixture into dots, you can even just place it in a small bowl and eat it like ice cream! It's delicious, quick, and healthy!

Chapter 4
STORY TIME SNACKS

Cat in the Hat Cookies

Sheep Cupcakes

Princess Wand Sugar Cookie Sticks

Pilgrim Hats

Turkey Veggie Cup

Nutter Butter Ice Cream Cones

Fruit Rainbow Cup

Graham Cracker Airplane

Oreo Puppies

Oreo Hedgehogs

Valentine's Day Lollipops

{ Cat in the Hat Cookies }

Kids love Dr. Seuss's *Cat in the Hat* and, if your kids are anything like mine, they'll just about flip over these fun cookie hats. Putting these cookies together is a great way to help kids practice their building skills while enjoying a delicious treat. The colorful banana and strawberries stripes are so fun!

YIELDS 6 CAT IN THE HAT COOKIES

3 Oreo cookies
5 strawberries, sliced vertically into 4–6 thin slices;
set aside the bottom tips of the strawberries
1 banana, sliced vertically into 12 thin slices

1. Carefully remove one side of your Oreo cookie with a knife. You don't need to worry about keeping the cream filling intact; you just don't want to break the cookie.

2. Place your Oreo cookie center side up on the table, then place a strawberry slice on top of the cookie, followed by a banana slice. Continue alternating the fruit until hat is your desired height. Place tip of a cut strawberry on top to finish the hat look.

3. Repeat with the remaining Oreo cookie halves and enjoy!

{ Sheep Cupcakes }

These little Sheep Cupcakes are white, puffy, and adorable! Topped with sweet mini marshmallows, they are a perfect cupcake idea for playdates or nursery rhyme–themed baby showers. This recipe uses Hershey's Kisses for the sheep's little heads, which makes for a delicious, extra chocolaty surprise.

YIELDS 24 CUPCAKES

½ batch Buttercream Frosting (see recipe in Chapter 1)

24 Perfect Chocolate Cupcakes (see recipe in Chapter 1), or cupcakes of your choice

24 Hershey's Kisses

48 candy eyes

2 (10.5-ounce) bags mini marshmallows

¼ cup light cocoa candy melts

48 mini chocolate chips

12 heart sprinkles, optional

1. Use a small spatula to add a thin layer of Buttercream Frosting to the tops of your prepared cupcakes; you will not use all of the icing.

2. Take the wrappers off of the Hershey's Kisses and place an upside-down Hershey's Kiss on the front edge of each cupcake.

3. Place a small amount of Buttercream Frosting on the back of the candy eyes and use it as a glue to adhere the eyes to the bottom of the Hershey's Kiss.

(Continued on next page) ▶

4. Place marshmallows on top of the cupcake surrounding the Hershey's Kiss, making sure to thoroughly cover the Buttercream Frosting.

5. Melt cocoa candy melts in a candy melting electric pot according to package instructions, or in the microwave at 30-second increments. Using a small toothpick and melted chocolate apply mini chocolate chips to the top of the Hershey's Kiss head. Using the toothpick and melted chocolate, draw on a smile directly below the eyes.

6. Repeat previous steps until you have 24 Sheep Cupcakes.

7. If desired, add heart sprinkles to the top of your Hershey's Kiss with a tiny amount of Buttercream Frosting to half of your sheep to divide them into girls and boys.

{ Princess Wand Sugar Cookie Sticks }

Growing up, my sisters and I loved princess movies. These Princess Wand Sugar Cookie Sticks remind me of days that were filled with yellow ball gowns and dancing with a beast, fun under the sea with a fish as our best friend, and patiently waiting for our Prince Charmings to come. These treats are guaranteed to pique your kids' imaginations and take them to courtyards, palaces, and mysterious worlds where anything can happen. Let your kids help you make these cookies and enjoy the magic carpet ride!

YIELDS 12 PRINCESS WAND COOKIES

1 batch Sugar Cookie dough (see recipe in Chapter 1)

Cookie cutters; use ones shaped like crowns, shoes, stars, or anything else your child loves

1 batch Cookie Glaze Icing (see recipe in Chapter 1)

12 (8-inch) cookie sticks, found in your local craft store

2–3 drops AmeriColor or Wilton coloring gel in any color or colors you desire

Sprinkles, candy, or other edible embellishments, optional

12 (10-inch) ribbons, optional

1. Preheat oven to 375°F.

2. To make your cookies, roll out the cookie dough to about ½-inch thickness so the finished cookies won't break when the lollipop sticks have been placed in them. Use your cookie cutters to cut whatever shapes you'd like out of the dough. Next, insert the cookie sticks into the bottom of the cookies before baking for 10 minutes or until the edges are slightly golden. Note: You may only be able to bake a few cookies at a time depending on how large you make your cookies.

(Continued on next page) ▶

3. Separate icing into multiple bowls (one bowl per desired frosting color) if you will be using a couple different colors and then mix with coloring gels.

4. Place your colored glaze icing in cake-decorating bags with a #2 tip.

5. To decorate your cookies, choose an icing color and use it to outline two cookies at a time.

6. Go back and fill in the first cookie with the same color icing and then repeat with the second cookie. I like to only do two cookies at a time so the gel dries nicely and doesn't leave a ridge.

7. Allow the icing to dry at least 4–5 hours before you ice on your details.

8. Once the icing has dried, use different colored icings to create different designs and shapes on your cookies. Add sprinkles, candy, and other edible embellishments as desired and have fun! I also tied a pretty ribbon around the stick. Store any extra glaze in an airtight container.

TREAT TIPS!

If you're only making cookies for a small crowd and have some left over, pop any unglazed sugar cookies in the freezer for a fun snack or quick dessert for your next occasion. Don't freeze your cookies once they are frosted, however. The icing will get white spots and, although your cookies will most certainly still be edible, they won't look very pretty.

{ Pilgrim Hats }

Thanksgiving is such a fun holiday! Who doesn't love a day filled with food, football, fun, and being thankful for everything that's great in your life? And these Pilgrim Hats will make this holiday even more enjoyable for your kids! This treat, which will inspire a discussion about the first Thanksgiving, is perfect for Pilgrim day at school or as favors for the kids' table at Thanksgiving dinner!

1 (1-pound) bag light cocoa candy melts

6 Oreo cookies

6 mini Reese's Peanut Butter Cups

6 mini M&M's

1. Melt cocoa candy melts in a candy melting electric pot according to package instructions, or in the microwave at 30-second increments.

2. Dip Oreo cookies into chocolate with a candy melt dipping scoop or fork and cover completely. Place cookies on a piece of parchment paper or Silpat. Place in refrigerator until chocolate hardens, approximately 10 minutes.

3. Remove wrappers from peanut butter cups and dip into melted chocolate with a fork, covering them completely. Place a chocolate-covered peanut butter cup on top of each Oreo cookie.

4. Place a mini M&M on top of the Oreo cookie, in front of the peanut butter cup, for the hat buckle.

5. Place Pilgrim Hats in refrigerator until chocolate hardens, approximately 5 minutes.

{ Turkey Veggie Cup }

Help your picky eaters try some veggies with this fun and Thanksgiving Day–friendly Turkey Veggie Cup! This recipe includes green peppers, carrots, and a few of our family's other favorite veggies but you can use whatever your kids like—and maybe throw in a few more they haven't tried yet. After all, kids are more willing to try something if they think it's fun, which these Turkey Veggie Cups definitely are! So get your kids excited about Thanksgiving and let them enjoy the story of the holiday—one healthy veggie at a time!

YIELDS 1 CUP SLICED VEGGIES, SERVES 2

1 cup assorted veggies, cut into thin veggie sticks
1 (4" × 6") piece each of brown, orange, and red scrapbooking paper

2 googly eyes
Craft glue
Scotch Tape

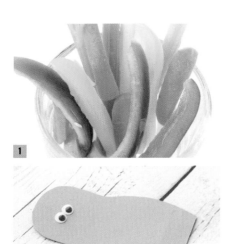

1. Place cut assorted veggies in a clear cup.

2. Cut the shape of a turkey's body and head, about 4–5 inches high, out of the brown scrapbook paper. Attach two eyes to turkey body with craft glue.

3. Cut a small, ¼-inch-wide, triangular-shaped beak out of your orange scrapbook paper and a small ¼-inch-long gobble out of your red scrapbooking paper.

4. Use the craft glue to attach the beak and gobble pieces to the center middle of the turkey head, then secure the turkey body to the front of the cup with a piece of tape.

{ Nutter Butter Ice Cream Cones }

Ice cream, Ice Cream, We All Scream for Ice Cream! When I was a little girl, I remember many ice cream outings with my grandparents. My siblings and I always looked forward to a cool, refreshing treat on some of the hottest summer days. For me, these ice cream Nutter Butters are a fun reminder of sweet days past, and hopefully they will be for you too! Let them inspire you to tell your kids some stories about your childhood—and how much you loved ice cream back in the day!

YIELDS 1 DOZEN NUTTER BUTTER ICE CREAM CONES

1 cup light cocoa candy melts

1 cup white chocolate candy melts

1 cup pink chocolate candy melts

12 Nutter Butter peanut butter sandwich cookies

2 tablespoons rainbow sprinkles

12 candy pearls

1. Melt your three candy melts in three separate bowls according to the package instructions, or in the microwave at 30-second increments.

2. Dip Nutter Butters into white chocolate halfway. Then, place them on a piece of parchment paper or Silpat and place in refrigerator until chocolate has hardened, approximately 5 minutes.

3. Dip Nutter Butters into the light cocoa candy melts, leaving approximately ⅓ of the white chocolate visible, and add sprinkles to the warm chocolate. Then, place them back in the refrigerator until chocolate has hardened, approximately 5 minutes.

4. Dip the tips of the Nutter Butters into the pink candy melts. Add sprinkles and a candy pearl on top of the warm pink chocolate. Place in refrigerator until chocolate hardens, approximately 5 minutes.

{ Fruit Rainbow Cup }

Rainbows are a perfect way to teach younger kids about colors and the world around them and, when you see one, it practically begs for a story! Use this Fruit Rainbow Cup to initiate a delicious story time for your kids. You'll find kiwi, strawberries, cantaloupe, and blueberries in this recipe that makes these cups fun *and* healthy! This is a perfect individual snack but can be made in a big bowl for parties too!

YIELDS 1 PARFAIT

⅓ cup fresh blueberries

⅓ cup diced strawberries

⅓ cup sliced kiwi, approximately 2 kiwis

⅓ cup sliced cantaloupe

2 tablespoons whipped topping such as Cool Whip, optional

Sprinkles, optional

1. Layer your fruit in a small parfait glass.

2. Top with whipped topping and sprinkles, if desired. Serve immediately.

{ Graham Cracker Airplane }

If you have kids, your life is likely surrounded by monster trucks, cars, and airplanes, just like mine!
If you have a hundred different types of transportation toys—and the books and stories that
go along with them—filling both your house and your children's imaginations, you're going to
love these Graham Cracker Airplanes! Just as fun to play with as they are to eat,
these planes are the perfect snack to help your kids
create some stories of their own.

YIELDS 1 CELERY STALK AIRPLANE

2 tablespoons peanut butter

1 celery stalk, washed and ends removed, plus 2 thin 2-inch-long pieces celery about ⅛ inch thick

1 toothpick

2 mini Reese's Peanut Butter Cups or Rolos

1 graham cracker, cut lengthwise

1. Spread your peanut butter on top of the celery stalk.

2. Insert toothpick horizontally through the celery stalk about 2 inches from one of the ends. Push the Reese's Peanut Butter Cups or Rolos onto the toothpick ends to create the airplane's wheels.

3. Place your graham cracker on top of your celery stalk directly above the airplane's wheels.

4. Create an X with your thin celery pieces and place them on the front of your airplane celery stalk, lightly pushing them into the peanut butter to help them stay in place.

{ Oreo Puppies }

These Oreo Puppies are adorable and perfect for any puppy-loving child. If you'd like,
you can add a little bow on the girl puppy's head and a brown eye patch on the boy puppy!
You can even add some fun black polka dots to the faces of the puppies to create Dalmatians,
perfect for a certain snack-time storybook!

YIELDS 6 OREO PUPPIES

1 cup white chocolate candy melts

6 Oreo cookies

1 cup light cocoa candy melts

¼ cup red chocolate candy melts

1. Melt your white chocolate candy melts in a candy melting electric pot according to the package instructions, or in the microwave at 30-second increments.

2. Dip your Oreo cookies into the white melted chocolate using a candy melt dipping scoop or fork, covering them completely. Place cookies on a piece of parchment paper or Silpat and place in refrigerator until chocolate hardens, approximately 10 minutes.

3. Melt your cocoa candy melts in a small bowl in the microwave at 30-second increments. Then, use a cake-decorating paintbrush and melted cocoa chocolate, to paint 2-inch-long ear shapes on a piece of parchment paper or Silpat. Place in refrigerator until chocolate has hardened, approximately 5 minutes. Use the melted light cocoa candy melts and a cake-decorating paintbrush to create a small circular brown eye patch for one of your puppies eyes if desired. Place back in refrigerator until chocolate hardens, approximately 2–3 minutes.

(Continued on next page) ▶

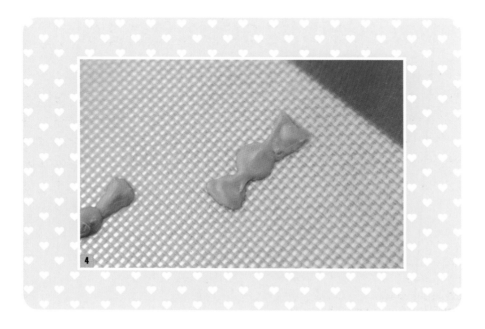

4. Melt your red chocolate candy melts in a small bowl in the microwave at 30-second increments. Repeat Step 3, but this time paint small ½-inch red bows by placing a single dot on the parchment paper and adding two triangle shapes to either side of the dot. Place in refrigerator until chocolate has hardened, approximately 5 minutes.

5. Attach the ears and bows to your chocolate puppies by using the melted cocoa chocolate and cake-decorating paintbrushes. Insert the ears into the sides of your Oreos and attach the bow on the top right-hand side of the Oreo. If you're using an eye patch, use the melted cocoa chocolate to place it under the spot where one of the eyes will go.

6. Using cake-decorating paintbrushes and melted cocoa and white chocolate, paint on the puppies' faces. Using the red chocolate candy melts, you can also add a small silly tongue. Place treats back in refrigerator until chocolate has hardened, approximately 2–3 minutes.

{ Oreo Hedgehogs }

Woodland creatures have become so popular today and it's no wonder! There is just something adorable about the little foxes, owls, and hedgehogs that fill your children's storybooks and daydreams. I was actually challenged by a few blogging friends of mine to create this little hedgehog and I just love how cute he turned out! And, just as little hedgehogs like to curl up, your children will love to snuggle up with these delicious treats as they settle down for story time.

YIELDS 12 OREO HEDGEHOGS

1 cup tan chocolate candy melts

1 cup light cocoa candy melts

1 batch Basic Oreo Bonbons, shaped as ovals and completed through Step 3 (see recipe in Chapter 1)

2 tablespoons chocolate sprinkles

12 mini chocolate chips

1. Melt both chocolate colors in two separate bowls according to the package instructions, or in the microwave at 30-second increments.

2. Use a fork to dip your Basic Oreo Bonbons halfway into tan candy melts. Place on a piece of parchment paper or Silpat and refrigerate until chocolate hardens, approximately 5 minutes.

(Continued on next page) ▶

3. Dip the other half of your bonbon in the light cocoa candy melts. While the chocolate is still warm, sprinkle on the brown sprinkles to give the bonbon a fur texture.

4. Using your light cocoa candy melts and a toothpick, draw two eyes on the center front of your Oreo Bonbon. Draw a mouth under the eyes. Then, "glue" on the mini chocolate chip that will form the nose by putting a small amount of melted chocolate on the bottom of it and placing it below the two eyes (see previous image). Place the bonbons back in the refrigerator until facial details are dry, approximately 2–3 minutes.

5. Repeat with remaining Oreo Bonbons until you have twelve little Oreo Hedgehogs.

{ Valentine's Day Lollipops }

These lollipops are a great gift for little kids to pass out to their friends, as the strawberry flavor in these lollipops adds the perfect touch for any special valentine. Tell your kids the story of Valentine's Day as you work together to make these sweet treats! You can even swap out the strawberry extract for mint extract for a cool winter flavor or you could add Christmas sprinkles for a great teacher's gift!

YIELDS 1 DOZEN LOLLIPOPS

2 cups sugar
⅔ cup light corn syrup
¼ cup water
Candy thermometer

2 teaspoons strawberry extract or extract of your choice
12 (6-inch) lollipop sticks
2 tablespoons assorted valentine sprinkles

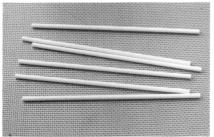

1. Line a cookie sheet with parchment paper or use a Silpat.

2. In a medium saucepan, combine sugar, corn syrup, and water. Bring to a boil stirring constantly.

3. Boil mixture for 5–7 minutes or until a candy thermometer reaches 310°F.

4. Remove mixture from stovetop and mix in strawberry extract. Allow to cool in the saucepan for 30 seconds to 1 minute.

5. Lightly pour liquid on the parchment paper to form small circles, then add lollipop sticks and sprinkles. The liquid will harden quickly so move fast.

6. Let lollipops cool completely, about 10–15 minutes, and carefully remove from parchment paper.

Chapter 5

SPOOKY BITES

Candy Corn Marshmallows

Monster Marshmallows

Ghost Sugar Cookies

Monster Rice Cereal Treats

Frankenstein Graham Crackers

Witch Cupcakes

{ Candy Corn Marshmallows }

These "boo" friendly Candy Corn Marshmallows are one of the easiest treats
you can make and only require a few ingredients. They make a super fun treat for
any candy-seeking trick-or-treaters and your kids are guaranteed to love them, too.

YIELDS 12 CANDY CORN MARSHMALLOWS

½ cup orange chocolate candy melts
12 marshmallows
½ cup yellow chocolate candy melts
½ cup brown chocolate candy melts

1. Melt your orange chocolate candy melts in a candy melting electric pot according to the package instructions, or in the microwave at 30-second increments.

2. Dip the bottom half of the marshmallow into the orange chocolate candy melts.

(Continued on next page) ▶

3. Place marshmallows in refrigerator until chocolate hardens, approximately 5 minutes.

4. Melt your yellow and brown chocolates as in Step 1. Dip the bottom of your orange-covered marshmallow in the yellow chocolate halfway to create a candy corn look. Place in refrigerator until chocolate has hardened, approximately 2–3 minutes.

5. Using a toothpick or the bottom end of a cake-decorating paintbrush and your brown chocolate candy melts, dot two eyes on your candy corn. Place marshmallows on a Silpat or parchment paper and place in refrigerator until chocolate has hardened, approximately 2–3 minutes.

{ Monster Marshmallows }

These marshmallows are an adorable treat that will let your kids' creativity fly! This recipe is
so easy for little kids to do and there's something so special about seeing the pride your children have
in their own monster creations. My little guy loved dipping marshmallows in the chocolate and then in
the sprinkles and he had a great time doing it! Which is just what your kids will have, too.

YIELDS 6 MONSTER MARSHMALLOWS

½ cup each blue, green, and yellow candy melts,
   or colors of your choice
6 lollipop sticks

6 marshmallows, nuts, or other toppings
¼ cup assorted sprinkles
18–20 candy eyes

1. Place your candy melts in three different bowls and melt according to package instructions or in the microwave at 30-second increments.

2. Insert your lollipop sticks into the bottom of your marshmallows.

3. Dip the bottom half of marshmallows into the melted candy melts in your desired colors.

4. Place your sprinkles, nuts, and other toppings in small bowls. While the chocolate is still hot, dip your marshmallows into desired sprinkles and add your candy eyes, as many as your child wants, by applying a small amount of melted chocolate to the back of the eye with a toothpick.

5. Place monster treats on a Silpat or piece of parchment paper and place in refrigerator until chocolate hardens, approximately 5 minutes.

{ Ghost Sugar Cookies }

These little ghosts are not spooky but friendly! They make a great gift for a Halloween school party and they look awesome when individually packaged and given as little treats! The ghost gets his fun shape from a tulip cookie cutter turned upside down and the candy eyes add a bit of personality that your kids will love!

YIELDS 12 GHOST SUGAR COOKIES

1 batch Cookie Glaze Icing (see recipe in Chapter 1)

1 batch Sugar Cookies (see recipe in Chapter 1), cut out using a tulip cookie cutter

24 candy eyes, found in craft stores

1. Place your Cookie Glaze Icing in a cake-decorating bag with a #2 tip.

2. To decorate your cookie, use your icing to outline two cookies at a time.

3. Go back and fill in the first cookie and then repeat with the second cookie. I like to only do two cookies at a time so the gel dries nicely and doesn't leave a ridge.

4. Repeat with all remaining cookies.

5. Allow cookies to dry for 2–3 hours. Place two eyes on each ghost cookie. The icing will still be tacky, so the eyes will stick well.

6. Allow cookies to dry overnight or until icing has completely hardened.

{ Monster Rice Cereal Treats }

Rice cereal treats are one of the easiest treats you can make, which is great because, when creating with kids, simple is always best. These Halloween-themed rice cereal treats put on a monster of a costume for the season and are a favorite among kids! Sometimes the best treats are the easiest—and the ones that are the most fun—to make.

YIELDS 12-18 MONSTER TREATS

3 tablespoons butter

1 (10-ounce) package marshmallows

6 cups Rice Krispies cereal

Cooking spray

1 tablespoon sprinkles

12-18 mini Oreo cookies

1 (3.5-ounce) tube black glaze icing gel

1. In a large saucepan, melt butter over medium heat. Add marshmallows and stir until completely melted. Remove from heat.

2. Add rice cereal to butter and marshmallow mixture and stir to combine.

3. Press mixture into a 13" × 9" pan coated with cooking spray. Sprinkle sprinkles on top.

4. Allow rice cereal to cool for about 10–15 minutes and then cut into 2–3-inch squares.

5. Separate your Oreos, trying to keep the cream on one side of the Oreo.

6. Using your gel icing as glue, glue the opened Oreo to the center top of the rice cereal treat. The cream side should be facing you. Apply a black dot of gel in the center of the cream to create an eyeball.

{ Frankenstein Graham Crackers }

These friendly Frankenstein Graham Crackers are the perfect addition to any kid's Halloween bash!
They come together quickly when you use the premade gel icing you can find in your
local craft store. I love the pop that the shimmer in the gel icing adds to this recipe
and the googly eyes bring these little Frankensteins to life.

YIELDS 6 FRANKENSTEIN GRAHAM CRACKERS

3 full chocolate graham crackers
1 tube green gel icing
12 candy eyes
2–3 tablespoons brown sprinkles

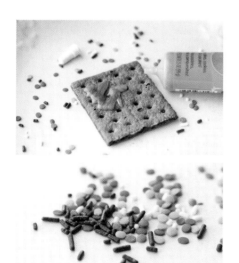

1. Break your chocolate graham crackers in half vertically.

2. Cover your graham crackers with green gel icing and spread evenly with a butter knife or small spatula.

3. Add your candy eyes to the center of Frankenstein faces. Use a small brown sprinkle for the mouth and add a few more sprinkles to the top of the Frankenstein head to create his hair.

{ Witch Cupcakes }

These little cupcakes are one of my all-time favorite Halloween treats. The cupcakes themselves are delicious and the legs are so easy to make out of paper straws that you can find at any craft store. You can choose from so many colors and designs that your kids, like mine, are guaranteed to cackle with happiness whenever you serve these for a snack.

YIELDS 2 DOZEN WITCH CUPCAKES

1 batch Buttercream Frosting (see recipe in Chapter 1)
1 batch Perfect Chocolate Cupcakes (see recipe in Chapter 1)
12 Oreo cookies
24 Hershey's Kisses

1 tube green gel icing
2–3 tablespoons sprinkles, divided
24 colorful paper straws
Craft glue
48 small feet, cut out of construction or scrapbooking paper

1. Place your Buttercream Frosting in a cake-decorating bag with a #1M tip. Pipe icing onto cupcakes.

2. Pull apart all Oreo cookies.

3. Place one Hershey's Kiss on the top of each half of the Oreo cookies, making sure the cream side is facing down. Outline all Hershey's Kisses with green gel icing and top with 1 tablespoon of sprinkles.

4. Place Oreo hat on cupcake at a slant.

5. Cut all paper straws in half and glue the feet onto the ends of the straws. Insert the straw legs into the center of each cupcake.

6. Top with remaining 1–2 tablespoons of sprinkles.

Chapter 6

PICNIC MUNCHIES

Oreo Bumblebees

Peanut Butter Cup Butterflies

Baby Chicks

Ice Cream Sandwiches

Watermelon Cupcakes

Flowerpot Cupcakes

Sports Balls Oreo Truffles

Easter Egg Nests

Peanut Butter Ritz Bunnies

{ Oreo Bumblebees }

These bumblebees are perfect for the hot summer days when you and your kids are out in the backyard all day. But you won't find your kids shooing away these busy bumblebees! Instead, you'll find yourself retreating to your cool kitchen and having fun whipping up these Oreo Bumblebees all summer long!

YIELDS 12 OREO BUMBLEBEES

1 (1-pound) bag brown chocolate candy melts

12 Oreo cookies

1 cup yellow chocolate candy melts

3 s'more-sized marshmallows

24 candy eyes

1. Melt brown chocolate candy melts according to the package instructions or in the microwave at 30-second increments.

2. Dip Oreo cookies into chocolate using a candy melt dipping scoop or fork, covering completely.

3. Place chocolate-covered Oreos on a piece of parchment paper or Silpat and place in refrigerator until chocolate hardens, approximately 10 minutes.

4. Repeat Step 1 with the yellow candy melts. Scoop melted chocolate into a cake-decorating bag with a #2 tip. Slowly pipe yellow lines on the Oreo body.

5. Cut marshmallow into five equal pieces lengthwise and then again widthwise.

(Continued on next page) ▶

6. Using the melted brown chocolate and cake-decorating paintbrushes, attach two marshmallow wings to the top center of each Oreo cookie at a 45-degree angle.

7. Using the melted yellow chocolate and cake-decorating paintbrushes, paint two ½-inch-long antennae for each bumblebee on a piece of parchment paper or Silpat. Place in refrigerator until chocolate has hardened, approximately 3 minutes.

8. Attach candy eyes and antennae in front of the marshmallow wings using the melted yellow chocolate and cake-decorating paintbrushes.

TREAT TIPS!

The wings in this recipe are made out of the s'mores marshmallows that are larger and are more square in shape, which helps give the wings a better shape. But, if you can't find the s'mores marshmallows in the store, you can easily make the wings out of the regular-sized marshmallows as well.

{ Peanut Butter Cup Butterflies }

Some of the best parts of spring are the fresh blooms and butterflies that make their long-awaited debut.
These Peanut Butter Cup Butterflies are a perfect treat to make in celebration of new beginnings.
The pretzel thins make the perfect wings and the colorful body
is a sugary sweet bite in your mouth.

YIELDS 4 BUTTERFLIES

4 full-sized peanut butter cups
¼ batch Buttercream Frosting (see recipe in Chapter 1)
8 pretzel thins
4 sugary gummy worms

1. Use a spoon to create a ¼-inch-thick line of frosting down the center of the peanut butter cups.

2. Place two pretzel thins at a 45-degree angle in the frosting on either side of the line of frosting on top of the peanut butter cup to look like wings.

3. Place a sugary gummy worm in between the pretzel wings and enjoy!

{ Baby Chicks }

Ever since my oldest son was born we've made sure to make Easter special. We always color eggs
and have an Easter egg hunt, and we've even had Easter egg hunts with his little buddies.
These Baby Chicks are perfect for an Easter get-together or for any little gathering for kids,
such as birthday parties, baby showers, or preschool graduations.
They are a yummy, fun treat that the whole family will love!

YIELDS 6 BABY CHICKS

1 (1-pound) bag yellow chocolate candy melts
¼ cup orange chocolate candy melts
¼ cup brown chocolate candy melts
6 Oreos

1. Melt yellow, orange, and brown chocolate melts in separate bowls according to
the package instructions or in the microwave at 30-second increments.

2. Dip your Oreo cookies in yellow chocolate with a candy melt dipping scoop or
fork and cover completely. Place cookies on a piece of parchment paper or Silpat
and place in refrigerator until chocolate hardens, approximately 10 minutes.

3. Using the bottom end of your cake-decorating paintbrush and brown chocolate,
dot two eyes on the center of the Baby Chick's face.

(Continued on next page) ▶

4. Using a small cake-decorating paintbrush and orange chocolate, paint on a triangular beak directly below the eyes. Use the yellow chocolate to add a small tuft of hair above the eyes.

5. Repeat with remaining Oreos, then place Baby Chicks back in the refrigerator until chocolate has hardened, approximately 5 minutes.

{ Ice Cream Sandwiches }

One of my little boys' favorite ice cream treats is an ice cream sandwich. We decided to make our own version one day and not only was it a refreshing treat but it was a fun, summertime activity that any kid can do! My little boys love being able to decorate their own food and this was a fun way they got to choose their favorite toppings.

YIELDS 6 COOKIE SANDWICHES

1 quart vanilla ice cream or flavor of your choice

1 cup peanuts

¼ cup rainbow sprinkles

½ cup semisweet chocolate chips

1 dozen of your favorite chocolate chip cookies, either homemade or store-bought (I love using the regular Chips Ahoy! cookies)

1. Place your ice cream on the counter and allow to soften slightly.

2. Crush the peanuts by placing them in a sandwich bag and lightly hitting them with a rolling pin or wooden spoon. Place crushed peanuts in a small bowl or plate, or in mini baking cups if you plan on having your kids decorate the cookies.

3. Place the sprinkles and semisweet chocolate chips in two separate small bowls, on two plates, or if your kids will be decorating, place them in two mini baking cups.

4. Using a small kitchen spatula, spread ice cream on the bottom of one cookie and place your second cookie on top of the first cookie facing up.

(Continued on next page) ▶

5. Roll the sides of the cookie in your desired topping. You can also have your kids use their hands to decorate their cookies.

6. Repeat with remaining cookies, then put them on a small plate and place in freezer until ice cream hardens again, about 15–20 minutes.

{ Watermelon Cupcakes }

It's not summertime without watermelons, right? Well, at least for my family it isn't. We love the sweet and refreshing taste of watermelon and have been known to eat a whole watermelon at one little family gathering. These cupcakes are so fun and will be perfect for your summertime bash as well! I used a strawberry cake mix for the cupcakes but if strawberry isn't your favorite you can use a white cake mix and add a bit of pink coloring gel.

YIELDS 24 WATERMELON CUPCAKES

1 batch Buttercream Frosting (see recipe in Chapter 1),
colored green (I used the Wilton coloring gel named "Leaf Green")
24 prepared strawberry cupcakes, made with a strawberry cake mix
¼ cup mini chocolate chips

1. Place colored Buttercream Frosting in a cake-decorating bag with a #1M tip. Pipe onto cupcakes.

2. Place mini chocolate chips on top of the icing to look like "seeds."

{ Flowerpot Cupcakes }

When my husband and I moved into our first home the first thing I wanted to do was plant a pretty flower garden in the front of our home. Now, the past few summers, I have two little helpers who love to pick the weeds and plant new flowers, also known as playing in the dirt and watching Mommy work. My little boys and I made some fun Flowerpot Cupcakes to finish up a fun day of play!

YIELDS 24 FLOWERPOT CUPCAKES

1 batch Buttercream Frosting (see recipe in Chapter 1) (I left mine white but you could also color it a light green to look like "grass")

1 batch Perfect Chocolate Cupcakes (see recipe in Chapter 1)

24 (6-inch) lollipop sticks

24 peach rings

48 jelly leaf candies; you could also use green Dots and shape them into leaves

Green sugar sprinkles, optional

1. Using a small spatula, spread your Buttercream Frosting on top of cupcakes.

2. Insert your lollipop sticks into the bottoms of the peach rings and cut your leaf candies in half to create two leaves.

3. Insert your lollipop stick into the center of the cupcake and place leaf candies on the frosting on opposite sides of the lollipop stick.

4. If desired, sprinkle with green sprinkles and remove the cupcake wrappers to allow the "dirt" to show through.

{ Sports Balls Oreo Truffles }

Living in a home with my husband and two little boys, there are always soccer balls being kicked, baseballs being tossed, or a sporting event being watched. These sports ball truffles are perfect for game day and are fun little treats for the sports-loving kids in your family.

YIELDS 12 SPORTS BALLS OREO TRUFFLES

1 cup white chocolate candy melts
1 cup orange chocolate candy melts
1 cup light cocoa candy melts
¼ cup red chocolate candy melts

12 Basic Oreo Bonbons, completed through Step 3, formed into your desired sports ball forms, and chilled (see recipe in Chapter 1)

1. Place your candy melts in four different bowls and melt in the microwave at 30-second increments.

2. Dip your Oreo Bonbons with a candy melt dipping scoop or with a fork into the melted chocolate depending on the type of ball being made. For example, dip the basketballs into the orange chocolate, the baseballs into the white, and the footballs into the brown. Place on a Silpat or piece of parchment paper and place in refrigerator until chocolate hardens, approximately 5 minutes.

3. Place remaining melted red, brown, and white chocolate in three different piping bags, each with a #2 tip. If you only have one #2 tip you will need to do one color at a time.

4. Using your piping bag, draw the corresponding lines on your bonbons. Use the white melted chocolate to decorate the footballs, the red chocolate to decorate the baseballs, and the brown chocolate to decorate the basketballs.

5. Place bonbons on a Silpat or a piece of parchment paper and place in the refrigerator until chocolate hardens, approximately 2–3 minutes.

{ Easter Egg Nests }

These Easter Egg Nests are so simple to make and are an adorable favor for the kids at dinnertime.
I love how the green-colored coconut flakes add a fun pop of color to these pastel treats.
If you want to mix things up, feel free to swap out the Easter egg candies for a sugary Peep!

YIELDS 10 SMALL EASTER EGG NESTS

¼ cup butter

1 (10-ounce) bag of marshmallows

5 cups of rice cereal

½ cup shredded coconut flakes

1–2 drops Wilton Green coloring gel

10–30 Easter egg candies, such as Whoppers Robin Eggs
(Note: Amount will depend on how many eggs you want in each nest. Three egg candies fit perfectly.)

1. Melt butter in a medium saucepan on medium-low heat.

2. Add marshmallows and stir until melted.

3. Pour melted marshmallows over cereal and mix until combined.

4. While rice cereal is still warm use your hands to form a small nest. I rolled the rice cereal into a ball and then used my thumbs to create an indent in the middle of the ball. My nests were about 4 inches wide but you can make them smaller or bigger.

5. Place nests on a piece of parchment paper or Silpat and allow to cool, approximately 5 minutes.

(Continued on next page) ▶

6. Mix coconut flakes and green color gel in a small bowl with your fingers until all flakes are colored green.

7. Place a tablespoon of coconut flakes into each nest. You may need more or less depending on how big you made your nests.

8. Place Easter egg candies on top and serve.

{ Peanut Butter Ritz Bunnies }

Here's another springtime treat that is perfect for the little ones in your life. These little bunnies are made out of one of my favorite treats, peanut butter sandwiched between two Ritz crackers. But this recipe takes this delicious treat one step farther and covers the peanut butter sandwich in melted chocolate. You just can't go wrong with peanut butter and chocolate and these bunnies are so cute that your kids will be asking for them year round!

YIELDS 12 RITZ BUNNIES

½ cup peanut butter
24 Ritz crackers
1 (1-pound) bag brown chocolate candy melts
12 mini marshmallows

1. Using a small spatula or knife, spread a small amount of peanut butter on twelve Ritz crackers. Place the other twelve crackers on top.

2. Melt chocolate candy melts in a candy melting electric pot according to the package instructions, or in the microwave at 30-second increments.

3. Dip Ritz sandwiches in melted chocolate with candy melt dipping scoop or fork and cover completely. Remove Ritz sandwiches from melted chocolate with a candy melt dipping scoop or fork and tap edge lightly to remove any excess.

4. Place Ritz sandwiches on a piece of parchment paper or Silpat and refrigerate until chocolate hardens, approximately 10 minutes.

(Continued on next page) ▶

5. On a Silpat or piece of parchment paper, paint a 2–3-inch-long circular bunny's head with two 1–2-inch-long ears at the top using the melted chocolate and cake-decorating paintbrushes. Place in refrigerator until chocolate hardens, approximately 5 minutes.

6. Using the melted chocolate as glue, stick the bunny's head to the top back of the Ritz sandwich and the mini marshmallow to the bottom front of the Ritz sandwich to create a tail.

7. Repeat with remaining chocolate-covered sandwiches and place in refrigerator until chocolate has hardened, approximately 5 minutes. Enjoy!

Chapter 7

SNOWBALL FIGHT TREATS

Santa Hats

Christmas Tree Brownies

Rice Cereal Ornaments

Snowflake Cupcakes

Gingerbread Cookies

Snowman Cupcakes

Oreo Penguins

Polar Bear Oreos

Love Bug Oreos

{ Santa Hats }

Watch your kids' eyes light up when they see these fun strawberry Santa Hats!
The holidays are hectic so the fact that these quick and easy treats require only three
ingredients will put them at the top of your "nice" list! I loved using the colorful holiday sprinkles
to decorate the hat, but you could also use glittery white sprinkles as well!

YIELDS 10 SANTA HATS

....

1 cup white chocolate candy melts
10 strawberries
2–3 tablespoons sprinkles, optional
10 mini white marshmallows

....

1. Melt white chocolate candy melts in a candy melting electric pot according to the package instructions, or in the microwave at 30-second increments.

2. Use a knife to slice off the leafy top of the strawberry and discard. Dip the freshly cut top of the strawberry into the melted white chocolate.

(Continued on next page) ▶

3. Dip the warm, chocolate-covered strawberry bottom into the sprinkles and use your hand to slightly press sprinkles into the chocolate. Place the strawberry, sprinkle side down, on a piece or parchment paper or Silpat and refrigerate until chocolate hardens, approximately 5 minutes.

4. Using a small amount of melted chocolate, dip your mini marshmallows into the melted chocolate and place on top of the strawberries. Place strawberries back onto a Silpat or piece of parchment paper and place in refrigerator until chocolate hardens, approximately 2–3 minutes.

{ Christmas Tree Brownies }

One of my favorite chocolaty go-to treats for the kids is the classic brownie, and these Christmas Tree Brownies take a simple treat up a notch! This recipe is simple, but your kids will still have a blast creating festive trees adorned with their favorite colors and sprinkles.

YIELDS 8-10 CHRISTMAS TREE BROWNIES

1 box brownie mix
Triangle cookie cutter
1 tube red gel icing
1 tube green gel icing
Sprinkles, optional

1. Prepare brownies according to box directions, then set aside to cool.

2. Once brownies have cooled, use a triangle cookie cutter to cut out tree shapes.

3. Decorate using gel icing and sprinkles, if desired. I like to use the green icing to create tree branches and the red icing to form small ornaments. Let your kids be as creative as they want!

{ Rice Cereal Ornaments }

These Rice Cereal Ornaments give you a delicious treat and an interactive holiday activity all in one! Just shape the ornaments from the rice cereal ahead of time, place some fun small candies in prep bowls and a few gel icing tubes on the table, and the kids will have a blast decorating their own Christmas ornaments.

YIELDS 6-8 RICE CEREAL ORNAMENTS

¼ cup butter

1 (10-ounce) bag of marshmallows

5 cups of rice cereal

Ornament- or circle-shaped cookie cutter

3–4 gel icing tubes, in your favorite colors
(I love to use green, red, black, and yellow)

1 (1.69-ounce) bag of M&M's; amount per treat
is determined by what size ornaments you make

1. Melt butter in a medium saucepan on medium-low heat.

2. Add marshmallows and stir until melted.

3. Pour melted marshmallows over cereal and mix until combined.

4. Place warm rice cereal mix in an 8" × 10" baking pan and allow to cool, approximately 5–10 minutes.

5. Cut your rice cereal with an ornament or circle cookie cutter.

6. Using gel icing, decorate as desired. To add the M&M's to the ornaments, just use a few dots of gel icing as a glue.

{ Snowflake Cupcakes }

There is just something so beautiful about freshly fallen snow! But even if you don't live in a snowy locale, these cupcakes are perfect for any winter party. The vanilla candy snowflake on top adds an elegant touch and you won't believe how simple they are to make! Your kids will find themselves wishing for a snow day when they discover these fun and easy Snowflake Cupcakes!

YIELDS 24 SNOWFLAKE CUPCAKES

1 batch Buttercream Frosting (see recipe in Chapter 1), with 1–2 drops of AmeriColor Mint Green food coloring

1 batch Perfect Chocolate Cupcakes (see recipe in Chapter 1)

½ cup vanilla candy melts

Snowflake template printed on printer paper (I just Googled "snowflake template" and found one that I liked, opened it in a Word document, sized it down to the size I wanted my snowflake to be, and printed it!)

1. Place your Buttercream Frosting in a cake-decorating bag with a #1M tip. Pipe frosting on top of cupcakes.

2. Melt vanilla candy melts in a candy melting electric pot according to package instructions, or in the microwave at 30-second increments. Place melted chocolate in a cake-decorating bag with a #1 tip.

3. Slide your snowflake template underneath a piece of parchment paper and pipe a snowflake shape with your melted chocolate following the lines.

(Continued on next page) ▶

4. Place vanilla candy snowflakes in the refrigerator until chocolate has hardened, approximately 5 minutes.

5. Place vanilla candy snowflakes on top of cupcakes and serve!

TREAT TIPS!

These Snowflake Cupcakes would look so pretty in any one of your favorite colors! Feel free to swap out the mint green food coloring for whatever matches your holiday gathering.

{ Gingerbread Cookies }

The aroma of ginger, molasses, and cinnamon always fills the house during the holidays and these Gingerbread Cookies are a classic family favorite. Use the Cookie Glaze Icing to add silly faces and "clothes" to your gingerbread men and to make your snowflake gingerbread cookies (made with a flower cookie cutter) beautiful.

YIELDS 18 MEDIUM-SIZED COOKIES

½ cup butter
½ cup sugar
½ cup molasses
1 egg yolk
2 cups flour

½ teaspoon salt
½ teaspoon baking powder
½ teaspoon baking soda
½ teaspoon cinnamon
1 teaspoon cloves

1 teaspoon ginger
½ teaspoon nutmeg
1 batch Cookie Glaze Icing
  (see recipe in Chapter 1)

1. Cream together butter and sugar in a stand mixer or large bowl.

2. Add molasses and egg yolk.

3. In a medium bowl, combine remaining ingredients.

4. Add flour mixture to butter mixture and slowly mix together until ingredients are incorporated. Form the dough in a ball and keep in bowl; place in refrigerator for 1 hour.

5. Preheat oven to 350°F. Then, roll dough to ¼ inch thick and cut with your desired cookie cutters. I love to use snowflakes and the classic gingerbread cookie cutters, but you can use your favorite Christmas cookie cutters like bells, trees, and more.

6. Place cookies 2 inches apart on a baking sheet.

7. Bake for 8–10 minutes or until edges are slightly brown. Remove from oven and allow cookies to completely cool before icing.

(Continued on next page) ▶

8. Add Cookie Glaze Icing to a cake-decorating bag with a #2 tip. Ice cookies as desired. I love the classic gingerbread look with two eyes and three button dots down the center of the gingerbread. We also love to add clothing by drawing on shirts and pants.

9. Allow icing to dry for 4–5 hours before serving.

TREAT TIPS!

Place your iced Gingerbread Cookies in a clear gift bag and tie it closed with a pretty ribbon to make a great gift for friends and family! Just make sure you let the Cookie Glaze Icing icing dry overnight before placing them in the bag.

{ Snowman Cupcakes }

What little kid doesn't want to build a snowman? I remember many snow days filled with sledding down hills, snowball fights, and building snowmen with some of my and my siblings' closest friends. The cold never seemed to bother us when we were younger. These little Snowman Cupcakes are the perfect treat to make with your little ones to celebrate the magic and fun of the winter season. Kids will have a blast adding the snowman's nose and pretzel stick arms!

YIELDS 12 SNOWMAN CUPCAKES

½ batch Buttercream Frosting (see recipe in Chapter 1)

½ batch Perfect Chocolate Cupcakes (see recipe in Chapter 1)

6 orange Starburst or orange Tootsie Roll candies

24 pretzel sticks

72 mini chocolate chips

1. Place Buttercream Frosting in a cake-decorating bag with a #1M tip and pipe onto cupcakes.

2. Cut Starburst or Tootsie Roll in half and use your fingers to form a carrot nose shape. Place nose just off the center of the cupcake.

3. Add pretzel sticks to both sides of the nose at a 45-degree angle to form the snowman's arms.

4. Add two mini chocolate chips to the top center of the cupcake for eyes and four or five mini chocolate chips below the nose to make a mouth.

5. Repeat with remaining ingredients until you have twelve Snowman Cupcakes.

{ Oreo Penguins }

Growing up, my sister Courtney and I shared a room and her bed was always filled with soft, stuffed penguins! Anytime I see a penguin—stuffed or not—I think of my sister. While I made these Oreo treats just for her, they are perfect for the penguin lover in your life, too. Whether you're riding out a winter storm or just chilling out on a weekend, these Oreo Penguins are guaranteed to hit the spot!

YIELDS 6 OREO PENGUINS

½ cup white chocolate candy melts
¼ cup orange chocolate candy melts
¼ cup brown chocolate candy melts
6 Oreo cookies
3 flower sprinkles, if you want to make girl penguins

1. Melt all three candy melts in separate bowls in the microwave at 30-second increments.

2. Using your cake-decorating paintbrush and melted white chocolate candy melts, paint a heart-shaped face on the top of your Oreo cookie. Place on a Silpat or piece of parchment paper and place in refrigerator until chocolate hardens, approximately 2–3 minutes. Repeat for remaining Oreos.

(Continued on next page) ▶

3. Using your cake-decorating paintbrush and the orange chocolate candy melts, paint an orange beak at the center of the Oreo cookie. Paint on two V-shaped feet at the bottom of the Oreo and on top of the white chocolate. Use the bottom of your cake-decorating paintbrush and brown chocolate candy melts to create two eyes above the beak. Repeat for remaining Oreos.

4. If you want to make girl penguins, add a small dot of melted chocolate to the back of a flower sprinkle and place at the top of the penguin's head.

5. Place your Oreo cookies back in the refrigerator until chocolate details harden, approximately 3 minutes.

{ Polar Bear Oreos }

These little polar bear treats are one of my favorite candy treats that I have created. The white sprinkles on top add the perfect amount of texture and detail to these friendly winter bears. Put these polar bears out with some hot cocoa and your kids will get lost in a magical winter wonderland!

YIELDS 6 POLAR BEAR OREOS

1 cup white chocolate candy melts
6 Oreo cookies
2–3 tablespoons white sprinkles
½ cup black chocolate candy melts
12 mini white marshmallows

1. Melt white chocolate candy melts in a candy melting electric pot according to package instructions, or in the microwave at 30-second increments.

2. Dip your Oreo cookies into the melted chocolate with a candy melt dipping scoop or fork, covering completely, and tap lightly to remove any excess.

3. While the chocolate is still hot, sprinkle white sprinkles on top of Oreo cookies until the top of the cookie is covered.

4. Place your Oreo cookies on a Silpat or a piece of parchment paper and place in refrigerator until chocolate hardens, approximately 5 minutes.

5. Melt black chocolate candy melts as in Step 1.

(Continued on next page) ▶

6. Dip the sides of the mini marshmallows into the melted white chocolate and apply to both sides of the chocolate-covered Oreo, about 1 inch apart, to create ears.

7. Using a cake-decorating paintbrush or toothpick and black melted chocolate, paint two circles in the middle of each ear. Add a nose, eyes, and mouth to each polar bear using the remaining black chocolate and cake-decorating paintbrush.

8. Place your Oreos in the refrigerator until all chocolate hardens, approximately 2–3 minutes.

{ Love Bug Oreos }

Love is in the air! These little love bugs are such a sweet treat for the little valentines in your life. The heart sprinkles add such a fun touch for the holiday that is all about hearts! Feel free to omit the hearts for a regular ladybug treat that would be great for the spring and summer seasons!

YIELDS 12 LOVE BUG OREOS

1 cup red chocolate candy melts
12 Oreo cookies
1 tube black gel icing

Valentine heart sprinkles
½ cup vanilla candy melts

1. Melt red candy melts in a candy melting electric pot according to package instructions, or in the microwave at 30-second increments.

2. Dip Oreos in melted red candy melts using a candy melt dipping scoop and cover completely. Place Oreo cookies on a piece of parchment paper or a Silpat. Place in refrigerator until chocolate has hardened, approximately 10 minutes.

3. Using your black gel icing, pipe on a circular head that covers the top ¼ of the Oreo cookie, then pipe a thin black triangle down the center of the Oreo cookie to create the classic ladybug look.

4. Using your black gel icing, place multiple dots on either side of the love bug's "wings" and place a small heart sprinkle on top of each black dot.

5. Repeat Step 1 with vanilla candy melts. Then, to create the love bug's eyes, add two small white dots on the head of ladybug. Add a smaller dot of black gel icing on top.

6. Repeat with remaining chocolate-covered Oreos, place them on a Silpat or piece of parchment paper, and place in refrigerator until chocolate hardens, approximately 5 minutes. Enjoy!

Appendix

U.S./METRIC CONVERSION CHARTS

VOLUME CONVERSIONS

U.S. Volume Measure	Metric Equivalent
⅛ teaspoon	0.5 milliliter
¼ teaspoon	1 milliliter
½ teaspoon	2 milliliters
1 teaspoon	5 milliliters
½ tablespoon	7 milliliters
1 tablespoon (3 teaspoons)	15 milliliters
2 tablespoons (1 fluid ounce)	30 milliliters
¼ cup (4 tablespoons)	60 milliliters
⅓ cup	90 milliliters
½ cup (4 fluid ounces)	125 milliliters
⅔ cup	160 milliliters
¾ cup (6 fluid ounces)	180 milliliters
1 cup (16 tablespoons)	250 milliliters
1 pint (2 cups)	500 milliliters
1 quart (4 cups)	1 liter (about)

WEIGHT CONVERSIONS

U.S. Weight Measure	Metric Equivalent
½ ounce	15 grams
1 ounce	30 grams
2 ounces	60 grams
3 ounces	85 grams
¼ pound (4 ounces)	115 grams
½ pound (8 ounces)	225 grams
¾ pound (12 ounces)	340 grams
1 pound (16 ounces)	454 grams

OVEN TEMPERATURE CONVERSIONS

Degrees Fahrenheit	Degrees Celsius
200 degrees F	95 degrees C
250 degrees F	120 degrees C
275 degrees F	135 degrees C
300 degrees F	150 degrees C
325 degrees F	160 degrees C
350 degrees F	180 degrees C
375 degrees F	190 degrees C
400 degrees F	205 degrees C
425 degrees F	220 degrees C
450 degrees F	230 degrees C

BAKING PAN SIZES

U.S.	Metric
8 x 1½ inch round baking pan	20 x 4 cm cake tin
9 x 1½ inch round baking pan	23 x 3.5 cm cake tin
11 x 7 x 1½ inch baking pan	28 x 18 x 4 cm baking tin
13 x 9 x 2 inch baking pan	30 x 20 x 5 cm baking tin
2 quart rectangular baking dish	30 x 20 x 3 cm baking tin
15 x 10 x 2 inch baking pan	30 x 25 x 2 cm baking tin (Swiss roll tin)
9 inch pie plate	22 x 4 or 23 x 4 cm pie plate
7 or 8 inch springform pan	18 or 20 cm springform or loose bottom cake tin
9 x 5 x 3 inch loaf pan	23 x 13 x 7 cm or 2 lb narrow loaf or pâté tin
1½ quart casserole	1.5 liter casserole
2 quart casserole	2 liter casserole

INDEX

A

Animal Crackers, 59

B

Baby Chicks, 118–20

Baking pan sizes, 161

Baking sheets, 17

Balloon Sugar Cookies, 53–55

Basic recipes, 17–27

    Basic Oreo Bonbons, 26–27

    Buttercream Frosting, 19

    Cookie Glaze Icing, 21

    Perfect Chocolate Cupcakes, 22–23

    Sugar Cookies, 25

Beachy Creamsicle Cupcakes, 47–48

Blueberries. *See also* Strawberries

    Fruit Rainbow Cup, 87

    Yogurt Dots, 69–70

Boat Cupcakes, 43–45

Bonbons

    Basic Oreo Bonbons, 26–27

    Monkey Oreo Bonbons, 63–65

    Oreo Hedgehogs, 93–95

    Sports Balls Oreo Truffles, 128–29

Brownies, Christmas Trees, 141

Bumblebee Oreos, 113–15

Buttercream Frosting, 19

C

Cake-decorating bags, 16

Cake-decorating paintbrushes, 17

Cake-decorating paint set, 17

Cake-decorating tips, 16

Cakes. *See* Cupcakes

Candy Corn Marshmallows, 99–101

Candy melt dipping scoop, 16

Candy melting electric pot, 16

Candy melts, 16

Cat in the Hat Cookies, 73

Cereal Treats

    Easter Egg Nests, 131–32

    Monster Rice Cereal Treats, 106–7

    Rice Cereal Ornaments, 143

Chocolate Chip Cookies, 121–23

Chocolate Cupcakes. *See also* Cupcakes

    Boat Cupcakes, 43–45

    Flowerpot Cupcakes, 127

    Perfect Chocolate Cupcakes, 22–23

    Sheep Cupcakes, 75–76

Snowflake Cupcakes, 145–46

Snowman Cupcakes, 151

Witch Cupcakes, 110–11

Christmas Rice Cereal Ornaments, 143

Christmas Tree Brownies, 141

Cinnamon Sugar Tortilla Fish, 49–51

Circus Party Popcorn, 59

Circus Snacks, 52–70

Balloon Sugar Cookies, 53–55

Circus Party Popcorn, 59

Colorful Yogurt Dots, 69–70

Cotton Candy Cone Sugar Cookies, 61–62

Lion Crackers and Cheese, 56–57

Monkey Oreo Bonbons, 63–65

Rainbow Coated Pretzels, 66–67

Conversion charts, 160–61

Cookie Glaze Icing, 21

Cookies

Baby Chicks, 118–20

Basic Oreo Bonbons, 26–27

Bumblebee Oreos, 113–15

Cat in the Hat Cookies, 73

Chocolate Chip Cookies, 121–23

Christmas Tree Brownies, 141

Cookie Glaze Icing, 21

Crab Oreos, 29–31

Easter Egg Nests, 131–32

Frankenstein Graham Crackers, 109

Frog Oreos, 35–36

Ghost Sugar Cookies, 105

Gingerbread Cookies, 147–49

Hedgehog Oreos, 93–95

Ice Cream Sandwiches, 121–23

Love Bug Oreos, 159

Monkey Bonbons, 63–65

Monster Rice Cereal Treats, 106–7

Nutter Butter Ice Cream Cones, 84–85

Oreo Baby Chicks, 118–20

Oreo Bonbons Basic Recipe, 26–27

Oreo Bumblebees, 113–15

Oreo Crabs, 29–31

Oreo Frogs, 35–36

Oreo Hedgehogs, 93–95

Oreo Love Bugs, 159

Oreo Monkeys, 63–65

Oreo Penguins, 153–54

Oreo Pirates, 40–42

Oreo Polar Bears, 155–57

Oreo Puppies, 91–92

Oreo Sports Balls Truffles, 128–29

Oreo Turtles, 37–39

Penguin Oreos, 153–54

Pilgrim Hats, 80–81

Pirate Oreos, 40–42

Polar Bear Oreos, 155–57

Princess Wand Sugar Cookie Sticks, 77–79

Puppy Oreos, 91–92

Rice Cereal Ornaments, 143

Sports Balls Oreo Truffles, 128–29

Sugar Cookie Balloons, 53–55

Sugar Cookie Cotton Candy Cones, 61–62

Sugar Cookie Ghosts, 105

Sugar Cookie Princess Wands, 77–79

Sugar Cookies Basic Recipe, 25

Turtle Oreos, 37–39

Cookie scoop, 16

Cotton Candy Cones Sugar Cookies, 61–62

Couplers, 17

Crab Oreos, 29–31

Crackers

Animal Crackers Circus Party Popcorn, 59

Graham Cracker Airplane, 89

Graham Cracker Frankenstein, 109

Ritz Crackers Lion and Cheese, 56–57

Ritz Crackers Peanut Butter Bunnies, 133–35

Creamsicle Cream Cheese Frosting, 47

Creamsicle Cupcakes, 47–48

Cupcakes

Beachy Creamsicle Cupcakes, 47–48

Boat Cupcakes, 43–45

Chocolate Cupcake Perfect Recipe, 22–23

Creamsicle Cupcakes and Frosting, 47–48

Flowerpot Cupcakes, 127

Orange Cupcakes, 47–48

Perfect Chocolate Cupcakes, 22–23

Sheep Cupcakes, 75–76

Snowflake Cupcakes, 145–46

Snowman Cupcakes, 151

Strawberry Cupcakes, 124–25

Watermelon Cupcakes, 124–25

Witch Cupcakes, 110–11

D

Decorating bags, 16

Decorating tips, 16

Dipping scoop, 16

E

Easter Baby Chicks, 118–20

Easter Egg Nests, 131–32

Equipment, 15–17. *See also* Kitchen tools

F

Flowerpot Cupcakes, 127

Frankenstein Graham Crackers, 109

Frog Oreos, 35–36

Frostings

    Buttercream Frosting, 19

    Cookie Glaze Icing, 21

    Creamsicle Cream Cheese Frosting, 47

    gel icing colors, 17

Fruits

    Cat in the Hat Cookies, 73

    Colorful Yogurt Dots, 69–70

    Rainbow Fruit Cup, 87

    Santa Hats, 137–39

G

Gelatin Mason Jars, 32–33

Gel icing colors, 17

Ghost Sugar Cookies, 105

Gingerbread Cookies, 147–49

Graham Cracker Airplane, 89

Graham Cracker Frankenstein, 109

H

Halloween Treats

    Candy Corn Marshmallows, 99–101

    Frankenstein Graham Crackers, 109

    Ghost Sugar Cookies, 105

    Monster Marshmallows, 102–3

    Monster Rice Cereal Treats, 106–7

    Witch Cupcakes, 110–11

Hedgehog Oreos, 93–95

Holiday Treats. *See also* Halloween Treats

    Christmas Tree Brownies, 141

    Easter Baby Chicks, 118–20

    Easter Egg Nests, 131–32

    Gingerbread Cookies, 147–49

    Pilgrim Hats, 80–81

    Rice Cereal Ornaments, 143

    Santa Hats, 137–39

    Snowflake Cupcakes, 145–46

    Snowman Cupcakes, 151

    Turkey Veggie Cup, 83

    Valentine's Day Lollipops, 97

    Valentine's Love Bug Oreos, 159

I

Ice Cream Sandwiches, 121–23

Icing

Buttercream Frosting, 19

Cookie Glaze Icing, 21

Creamsicle Cream Cheese Frosting, 47

gel icing colors, 17

K

Kitchen tools, 15–17

cake-decorating bags, 16

cake-decorating paint set, 17

cake-decorating tips, 16

candy melt dipping scoop, 16

candy melting pot, 16

candy melts, 16

cookie scoop, 16

couplers, 17

gel icing colors, 17

parchment paper, 17

silicone baking sheets, 17

sprinkles, 17

L

Lion Crackers and Cheese, 56–57

Lollipops, 97

Love Bug Oreos, 159

M

Marshmallows

Candy Corn Marshmallows, 99–101

Easter Egg Nests, 131–32

Monster Marshmallows, 102–3

Monster Rice Cereal Treats, 106–7

Oreo Bumblebees, 113–15

Peanut Butter Ritz Bunnies, 133–35

Polar Bear Oreos, 155–57

Rice Cereal Ornaments, 143

Santa Hats, 137–39

Sheep Cupcakes, 75–76

Melting pot, 16

Monkey Oreo Bonbons, 63–65

Monster Marshmallows, 102–3

Monster Rice Cereal Treats, 106–7

N

Nutter Butter Ice Cream Cones, 84–85

O

Orange Cupcakes, 47–48. *See also* Cupcakes

Oreo Baby Chicks, 118–20

Oreo Bonbons Basic Recipe, 26–27

Oreo Bumblebees, 113–15

Oreo Crabs, 29–31

Oreo Frogs, 35–36

Oreo Hedgehogs, 93–95

Oreo Love Bugs, 159

Oreo Monkeys, 63–65

Oreo Penguins, 153–54

Oreo Pirates, 40–42

Oreo Polar Bears, 155–57

Oreo Puppies, 91–92

Oreo Sports Balls Truffles, 128–29

Oreo Turtles, 37–39

Ornaments Rice Cereal Treats, 143

Oven temperature conversions, 161

P

Paintbrushes, 17

Paint set, 17

Parchment paper, 17

Peanut Butter Cup Butterflies, 117

Peanut Butter Ritz Bunnies, 133–35

Penguin Oreos, 153–54

Perfect Chocolate Cupcakes, 22–23

Picnic Munchies, 112–35

    Baby Chicks, 118–20

    Easter Egg Nests, 131–32

    Flowerpot Cupcakes, 127

    Ice Cream Sandwiches, 121–23

    Oreo Bumblebees, 113–15

    Peanut Butter Cup Butterflies, 117

    Peanut Butter Ritz Bunnies, 133–35

    Sports Balls Oreo Truffles, 128–29

    Watermelon Cupcakes, 124–25

Pilgrim Hats, 80–81

Pirate Oreos, 40–42

Polar Bear Oreos, 155–57

Popcorn Circus Party, 59

Pretzels

    Oreo Frogs, 35–36

    Peanut Butter Cup Butterflies, 117

    Rainbow Coated Pretzels, 66–67

    Snowman Cupcakes, 151

Princess Wand Sugar Cookie Sticks, 77–79

Puppy Oreos, 91–92

R

Rainbow Coated Pretzels, 66–67

Rainbow Fruit Cup, 87

Rainbow sprinkles, 17

Rice Cereal Treats

    Easter Egg Nests, 131–32

    Monster Rice Cereal Treats, 106–7

    Rice Cereal Ornaments, 143

Ritz Crackers Lion and Cheese, 56–57

Ritz Crackers Peanut Butter Bunnies, 133–35

S

Santa Hats, 137–39

Sea Treats, 28–51

    Beachy Creamsicle Cupcakes, 47–48

    Boat Cupcakes, 43–45

    Cinnamon Sugar Tortilla Fish, 49–51

    Oreo Crabs, 29–31

    Oreo Frogs, 35–36

    Oreo Turtles, 37–39

    Pirate Oreos, 40–42

    Underwater Gelatin Mason Jars, 32–33

Sheep Cupcakes, 75–76

Silicone baking sheets, 17

Silpat, 17

Snowball Fight Treats, 136–59

    Christmas Tree Brownies, 141

    Gingerbread Cookies, 147–49

    Love Bug Oreos, 159

    Oreo Penguins, 153–54

    Polar Bear Oreos, 155–57

    Rice Cereal Ornaments, 143

    Santa Hats, 137–39

    Snowflake Cupcakes, 145–46

    Snowman Cupcakes, 151

Snowflake Cupcakes, 145–46

Snowman Cupcakes, 151

Spooky Bites, 98–111

    Candy Corn Marshmallows, 99–101

    Frankenstein Graham Crackers, 109

    Ghost Sugar Cookies, 105

    Monster Marshmallows, 102–3

    Monster Rice Cereal Treats, 106–7

    Witch Cupcakes, 110–11

Sports Balls Oreo Truffles, 128–29

Sprinkles, 17

Story Time Snacks, 71–97

    Cat in the Hat Cookies, 73

    Fruit Rainbow Cup, 87

    Graham Cracker Airplane, 89

Nutter Butter Ice Cream Cones, 84–85

Oreo Hedgehogs, 93–95

Oreo Puppies, 91–92

Pilgrim Hats, 80–81

Princess Wand Sugar Cookie Sticks, 77–79

Sheep Cupcakes, 75–76

Turkey Veggie Cup, 83

Valentine's Day Lollipops, 97

Strawberries. *See also* Blueberries

    Cat in the Hat Cookies, 73

    Fruit Rainbow Cup, 87

    Santa Hats, 137–39

Strawberry Cupcakes, 124–25. *See also* Cupcakes

Sugar Cookie Balloons, 53–55

Sugar Cookie Cotton Candy Cones, 61–62

Sugar Cookie Ghosts, 105

Sugar Cookie Princess Wands, 77–79

Sugar Cookies Basic Recipe, 25

Supplies, 15–17. *See also* Kitchen tools

T

Tips, 14–17

Tools, 15–17. *See also* Kitchen tools

Tortilla Cinnamon Sugar Treats, 49–51

Turkey Veggie Cup, 83

Turtle Oreos, 37–39

U

Underwater Gelatin Mason Jars, 32–33

V

Valentine's Day Lollipops, 97

Valentine's Love Bug Oreos, 159

Veggie Cup, 83

Volume conversions, 161

W

Watermelon Cupcakes, 124–25

Weight conversions, 161

Witch Cupcakes, 110–11

Y

Yogurt Dots, 69–70

ABOUT THE AUTHOR

Katie Wyllie is the creator of *Made to Be a Momma* (*www.madetobeamomma .com*), a blog where she shares recipes, do-it-yourself crafts, sewing tutorials, stories of motherhood, and her philosophy that making your house a home doesn't have to be expensive and yummy treats don't have to take hours to make. One of her favorite things to do in the kitchen is to create fun treats with her children. She enjoys the giggles and even the messes that come from their creative little minds.

Katie enjoys learning and expanding her photography skills by dabbling in family photography and spends some time being a second photographer for her sister, who is a professional photographer. Ultimately, her goal at *Made to Be a Momma* and in life is to inspire and encourage mothers in this blessed and sometimes messy life of motherhood. Katie is a Christian who lives in northeastern Pennsylvania, where she grew up, with her husband, Bryan, and their two little boys, Jacob and Carter.